10

A HILLSIDE HARVEST

A
HILLSIDE HARVEST

BY LANSING CHRISTMAN

Foreword by Carl Carmer

Illustrated by Ursula Suess

HANOVER HOUSE Garden City, New York

TO THE MEMORY
OF MY FATHER AND MOTHER
WILL AND CATHERINE CHRISTMAN

Who, these many years later, guide my footsteps
And my heart, and lead me warmly by the hand
To a higher, wider pastureland.

FOREWORD

THE BOZENKILL—"Drunkard Creek"—sings as it reels a crooked way through Lansing Christman's farm. It has a different song for each dawn and each dawn lights a different landscape for the farmer as he steps from his house into his dooryard.

One of Lansing Christman's gifts is that his eyes recognize the eternal newness of a countryman's day. The minuscule changes that occur in each fraction of that twenty-four hours are to him apparent and important. To his observing and poetic mind the coming of darkness is the ending of one season and the beginning of another.

The reader of these pages, be he countryman or one who has sometime lived on farmland, will be amazed that they contain so much that is at the same time familiar and magical. Let him step outside the farmhouse with Lansing Christman and there will stand the new-green elms—Kings of the Dooryard—and in the shade of one of them the forsythia will be displaying their gold below the royal purple of the lilacs. The day will open like a morning-glory and before the light is full Lansing Christman, standing beside the dooryard well, will have observed and felt the presence of a countless fellowship of recognizable plants, weeds, trees and birds. If the reader chooses to list them he will be surprised at the number of his own recognitions. For the first time, perhaps, he will have the gratifying sensation that, while he has not been aware of the impressions these have made on his mind, the impressions are there. All of these sights and sounds have been accents in his living and he needed beside him only this poet and philosopher to translate them into rich experience. Lansing Christman is master of facts that many regard as nature's commonplaces, but his mind and pen are ever proving that nature offers only the strange and wonderful.

Read these essays and you will become a convert to a creed implied but not enunciated. You will know, nevertheless, that Lansing Christman is happy on his brook-haunted acres, happy because "a man, imbued with the contentment of the harvest, knows that winds and rains can never chill the hearth of golden memories", happy because a countryman "knows the intimacy of the bird-songs that follow his labor, of strands of spider webs against the sunset sky, of the slow miracle of the curing hay in the sun", happy that though harvests be light they "can be rich in sun and song."

Conscious of these things, those who listen to this philosopher of the farm can believe he is sincere when he says that he would "wait for hours; he would wait for springs, even, for the flight-song of the woodcock, issued so richly and joyously from a sphere of stars" or that "all year long a countryman should reap from the spreading fields of the dawn, and the serene fields of the dusk. He should harvest from the day and its dark follower.".

Most of all, and without saying it directly, Lansing Christman emphasizes the spiritual necessity of man's dependence on nature. In an age when rhythms have been tortured into swift, nervous, and intolerable patterns his calm words prescribe that man be "awake to every chord and sound of the ever rhythmic hills." His unhurried prose suggests the measured and serene march of country days. To a diseased and fearful world this is good medicine.

Carl Carmer

OCTAGON HOUSE
IRVINGTON-ON-HUDSON

CONTENTS

CONTENTS

CONTENTS

xi

CONTENTS

A HILLSIDE HARVEST

DAWN AND
STARLIGHT

*I*T WOULD be well for a countryman, on this eve of the New Year, if he were to turn over a new leaf befitting his years of upland farm living. It would be well if he were to pledge himself anew to take in more that the good year yields in its four rich seasons that come in their turn with the "changing" sun over his woods and his hills.

The countryman who is in the habit of rising late may well resolve, as the old year ebbs, that he will rise with the sun on at least half the mornings of the year. Or, if he is the early rising countryman, who has seen much more of sunlit hours than those of stars, he may well say to himself that in this New Year he will become more intimate with the hours of darkness that come each night to his uplands.

Even a man familiar with years of mornings may well express his awe and delight at the break of each new day. There is, he says, a definite newness in each unfolding dawn. Though he may have seen the sun rise, morning after morning and year after year, there is new inspiration befitting this child of the day. So it is with the countryman who knows so well the darkened hours of night, hours that sparkle with stars, or shine with the faint gold of moonlight on the hills. A man knows the inspiration that the long nights yield, the mystery with which darkness seems to shroud the land. Perhaps a rabbit leaves its footprint in the snow in a pasture thicket, or maybe a grouse finds shelter under the boughs of the woodland pine. Perhaps a fox moves noiselessly across a wild pasture slope, or a deer moves in close to the orchard to feed on the frozen apples long since lost in the snow.

All these things belong to a man of hills. And if he will but reap, all these things are his harvest of sloping acres and woods. A man would do well to resolve that he will harvest from both the night and the dawn. He would resolve to become as familiar with the rising sun as he is with the last rich glow of light on afternoons. All year long he should reap from the spreading hills of the dawn, and the serene fields of the dusk. He should harvest from the day and its dark follower. A countryman should resolve to know more intimately the heartbeat of the hills in all their seasons and in all their precious hours.

MANY ARE THE SONGS

A MAN WHO has turned again to his work in the woods finds the hills changed from those he knew a few short months ago, changed from those October hills and those November fields. The green and the brown of the slopes have turned to white; the trees are leafless forms against the landscape. And the songs, too, have changed, for there are no robin carols nor running brooks; there are no cricket songs, nor thrushes.

The winter woods are like a new world to a man who is receptive to the songs and the beauty that take their turn to complete the cycle of the country year. He hears the clear song of the saw, or the sharp thud of the axe as it strikes into frosted wood. After a few strokes of the saw, or a few swings of the axe, he removes his coat or his jacket, and hangs it on a twig or a limb, nearby. He knows that woodcutting is hard work, that it exercises a man's muscles, and that it builds warmth, quickly, even against the zero days. Nor does he fear the wind, for winds have little success in penetrating the heart of the woodland. From day to day, he surveys the efforts of his harvest, and he sees the woodpiles growing more abundant along the winding roads between the ash and the oak and the beech.

Deep in the woods, the chickadees, especially, are old friends to a countryman. He has seen them turn, time and again, from caution to friendliness. He remembers standing like a silent figure among the trees, admiring the beauty of the woods, and the songs about him; he remembers how the birds flew down to alight on his wrists and arms, and his shoulders. At the slightest move, the birds would take to their wings again to give their pleasant chick-adee-calls from a nearby hemlock or an old maple. He hears the whirring wings of the partridge as it takes flight from under the sheltering hemlock boughs. He sees squirrels and rabbits and even the deer which had moved in close to feed on the swollen buds of the twigs and branches.

A countryman does not feel alone during these winter hours, even in the vast expanse of the wooded hills. He likes this part of winter, and the low sun, sending a rich spray of sunshine over the frozen leaves. He listens to the dried beech leaves, fingered by a falling snow, and talking in the wind. Many are the songs and the voices that build a lasting friendship between birds and trees and man. And once a man has been accepted into woodland ways, he feels that he belongs there, that he has become a part of the woods, like the trees, and that he is no longer a stranger to the woodpeckers and the nuthatches, and the chickadees.

A RAMBLE
IN THE WINTER

A WALK IN an upland pasture on any day in an open winter
may well bring new delight into a countryman's year. There is more
than the chill of the hour, a man thinks, and the full wealth of the
season may be gleaned on a slow ramble over the stones and the
mounds of his acres.

On the uplands, before a man enters his pine woods, he looks
back. The whole countryside seems to be at rest in its deep brown.
His wide sweeping view yields a picture of a field, framed by the
old stone walls that follow the land, up hill and down. The brown
reaches on, almost, into a vagueness made up of old strawberry
leaves and faded grass, and the stalks of the once brilliant goldenrod. It has shepherd's-purse and cinquefoil, and the fallen leaves of
the wild apple trees in the pasture. It has a thousand plants and
twigs and branches that have known the universal cycle of the seasons.

It is good for a man to feel the strength of the wind over the

7

browned carpet of the earth. Yet the pines bravely wear their garb of summer's green. When he steps into the swish and the roar of the boughs, moving in the wind, a man enters into a new world, a world all its own that lends satisfaction to his heart. He notes the bells of rain on the tips of the needles. He sees the chickadees, moving in song, among the swaying branches. And where a man has walked, a darker passage follows, for he brushes the boughs, and the raindrops slip with softness from the needles to the ground. They leave a stronger green in the wake of his casual walk.

When a man leaves his pines to step out into the open field once more, he sees where the "everlasting" stars the pasture slopes. The dry bloom tells him, with many other things, that winter can yield much more than cold and ice for a countryman. There is, for example, the miniature brook from last night's rain. The ledges hanging out over the stream guard it tenderly, as if the water moved with sureness toward the larger current of life. A man bends to touch his fingers to the icy coldness. He feels the chill blade of the wind against his unmittened hand. The brook, a man thinks, winds on into the lowlands like a silver vein, or like a silvered thread sewing the coats of the pasture together against the wind and the cold.

WINTER HAYMOW

A MAN, CLIMBING up the ladder into the mow to throw down hay for the horses and cows and sheep, may well pretend he is ascending one of his steep hillside meadows in the days of a summer harvest. With the sun streaming in through the cracks in the siding of the weathered barn, and with the faint sweet smell of hay and mints, a summer flavor seeps on into these days of snow.

The green of timothy, the yellow of the goldenrod, the white of the daisy, compact and preserved in the bed of the bay, are conspicuous in the sun's bright rays. He has, a man thinks, returned in some measure to a summer that has passed. The hay has been used down to the first beams, but a man is close enough to the slope of the roof to view the old and abandoned nests of the swallows in the peak of the barn, and the wasps' nests, plastered firmly and snugly against the rafters, and cobwebs, suspended from the hayfork in silvered strands.

Deep in winter, a man reflects on his summer harvest and the hot dry days of curing hay and locust songs. Those summer days were rushing hours of work; what a man missed then, he garners new

9

in winter's solitude. An old barn, rich in hay, rich in the simplicity of field and meadow harbored within its walls, is a good place for a man to find a summer richness that he brought in from the fields last June.

The sun streams in to brighten the colors in the mow. A man watches the dust rise from the hay and float in a shimmering wave through the beams of light across the bay. Some are diamond-shaped particles, it seems, etched in silver in the sun. High in the loft, secure from snow and wind, a man dips back into summer. Just as surely as the hay lowers from day to day in meeting the demands of the stock, he knows that these winter days will soften into spring. A man throwing down hay does more than bring sustenance to his Holsteins and his Guernseys, to his sheep, and the team of old grays. In every thought he finds nourishment for dreams; he finds nurture for a farm philosophy that makes all days good days, and all farm years good years to a countryman.

WINTER MORNING

A COUNTRYMAN, rising before the winter sun, to start his morning chores, finds a friendliness in the figure of the old barn, looming out through the darkness against the snow and the hills. He knows the warmth and the activity that will greet him as he opens the doors. The cows, hearing his approach, will rise in their stanchions in anticipation of their feeding; the horses will paw at the floor of their stalls.

When he drops the manger doors, both grays look out, expectantly, and neigh for their grain. It gives a man the feeling that they need him, and expect him. It builds richly into the satisfaction and the goodness of farm living. He is aware of that satisfaction when he pours the grain into the feed boxes, and forks the hay into the mangers. The horses fed, a man follows the alleyway into the cow stable, where the cows, big-eyed and kind, moo impatiently as he carries in the forkfuls of hay and cornstalks, and the measures of grain. They strain in their stanchions. Turning to the sheep shed, there is a scuffle of feet as a man throws in the hay; a race for the basins of oats. In the hen house, the chickens fly down from

11

their roosts as soon as he enters. Least patient of all, a man thinks, are the swine, racing for their troughs, and squealing beyond any point of complacency.

This is a routine procedure for a countryman. Each winter morning finds him retracing the same steps of the preceding dawn. But there is something about the sharp morning chill that he looks forward to, something that strengthens his sinews. He is intrigued by the calm of those winter dawns when there is no wind. He is intrigued by those mornings when a falling snow sweeps against his face as he walks to the barn. He likes the wind on those mornings when the strong gales brush over his fields. And he delights in the hour, at last, when the dawn comes, faintly at first, but with increasing glory in those minutes before the great ball of light shows itself over the cold eastern hills.

Routine though it is, a man can always find newness in the dawn, and in those trips to the barn, morning after morning. A man feels that the satisfaction that comes to his farm stock at feeding time, comes also to him. He has learned the ways of his cows and his horses, just as he has learned the ways of the snow and the wind. The feeding done, he hears the creaking of stanchions and the rustling of cornstalks and hay; he hears the grays munching their timothy; the ewes' rapid chewing. He hears the clucking of hens as they feed from the hoppers of scratch feed and mash. They are songs of gratitude that linger in his ears as he starts to the house for his breakfast by the fire. They are satisfying sounds to a man who rises before the winter sun to start his day in the breathing warmth of his upland barn. Filled with contemplation, a man knows that a lifetime of farm living will erase none of the expectancy that marks the coming of day. He knows that a lifetime of farm living will erase none of the beauty of the morning hills, none of the grace and loveliness of an old barn, magnificent, almost, in the coming dawn.

WALKING
IN WINTER NIGHT

A COUNTRYMAN, sometimes, will seek the friendliness of the winter night, seek it that he may know better the sounds and the moods that move in over his hills and valleys when the darkness comes. He knows little of it intimately, for most of his hours of dreams are spent indoors, in the warmth of a room, brilliant with light, friendly with voices and papers and books, and soft with music.

But let a man bundle up, and walk out into the winter night, into the darkness of it, into the strong northwest winds and the flakes of snow blown in with the diminishing flurries and squalls. It is a cold night, but a countryman faces it, for a mile, perhaps, with the only light that which comes from the soft glow of the moon breaking faintly through the clouds and the sheets of snow.

He walks a familiar road. Not a car nor a footman pass. A man is glad, for he finds that the wind is more friendly than he had expected. He hears it roar through the wooded hills. He hears the dried beech leaves talking. He hears the gusts move sharply through the reeds and the cattails. He hears the swaying boughs of the pine, the creaking and straining of the basswood and the oak. It is a friendly wind, he thinks. It gives him voices and music from the trees and the reeds, and the winter hills.

And it is a friendly night. It gives him the far-off whistle of the train, the call of the owl from an old apple tree in the pasture. It gives him the snow, the silhouettes of trees and old fences and darkened barn buildings. It yields brilliant streams of light, pouring out richly from the windows of the homes of his neighbors. He knows they are inviting lights, but he does not answer. Tonight he is part of the outdoors, a part of the hills and the trees, and the road. And when, at last, he steps softly back into the glowing rooms of his house, he smiles, for his heart is warm. He has found the night and its darkness as friendly as the rich glowing light of the day.

KING
OF THE DOORYARD

*D*OORYARD ELMS yield charm to countless lawns of villages and farms through all the seasons of the year. They are steadfast trees, breasting the flow of winds, reddening with the buds of spring, throwing summer canopies of shade over grass and walk and well. Two such elms have been a part of a countryman's lawn for a century of seasons. They have grown into giant trees, bowing to the storm, but lifting again their graceful arms to sun and stars. They are old trees, and broad, and great cables have been used to strengthen the upper branches against the sweeping gales, the heaviness of snow, and the silvered coverings of ice.

The elms have long been a part of a man's hills and the seasons. He likes to think that the trees, through their quiet eyes, have harvested much in their century-old reign of his dooryard. They have held the pouch-like nests of the oriole in many Junes. Their rough bark has been the harvesting ground for generations of nuthatches and woodpeckers, and squirrels have glided swiftly over their spreading limbs.

Like a mirror of the years, they have reflected the days of a hundred springs and summers, and a hundred golden falls. They have recorded the changing of the seasons, all the way from the leafless days of snow into the sharp crisp hours of another autumn when the fingers of frost tugged at the twigs to release the yellowed leaves in wind or in shower. They record for a man the sounds and the songs, the signs and the seasons.

The dooryard elms stand serenely like protecting sentinels by a countryman's house. A man and his family have grown to know the meaning and the worth of their year-long companionship, and the goodness of their friendly arms, throwing a fountain of shade against the noonday sun, building lovely and graceful forms against autumn and winter skies, a psalm of softness in the spring.

Listening to the humming of the boughs in the cold sharp winds, a countryman detects the surging chords building up into an upland melody, one that a man will remember. He will remember the songs and the carols that have poured out from the lofty limbs. He will remember the autumn hour of color, the great bare arms and hands when the leaves have gone. Even in their hour of snow, the elms are majestic trees. They have a right to be gracious and proud; they are king of a man's dooryard.

OF PEARLS AND SUN

A FREEZING RAIN can turn a countryman's world into a dream-like palace of fragile traceries and spires. The silvered garb of ice on the woodland slopes and hills can turn the uplands into richness and beauty, into deep and crystaled inspiration. The transformation may come quickly, overnight. Falling temperatures and a winter rain play their brilliant roles in the jeweled and glistening change. The hours of a serene silence come with the dawn, when the sun, pushing higher over the hills, hangs bright and glittering jewels on every bud and bough.

In this world of silence, and in this morning of ice, a man goes forth into his pastures and his fields where the night's storm, working hand in hand with the day's sun, has spread a panorama of gems and jewels upon the dried stalks of the goldenrod and grass, on bushes and thickets and trees. One goes quietly into his woods for a loveliness that has been sewn on every tree by the artistic and inspiring fingers of the season and the storm. Every branch and twig and bole is crowned and glazed in ice. The dried and browned leaf

17

of the beech, cased in pearl, shows with vivid clarity each vein and spire of the summer leaf.

A wooded path has been transformed into a hall of glass and pearls. It winds its way through the quietness of the glittering palace etched in ice and sun. The hemlock bows under the heaviness of its silvered drapes, while the sturdy pine points like a green-crystaled cone into the light that overspreads the land. The smooth-boled beech becomes a towering fountain caught in the midst of the brightening day. The birch wood is a fairyland of bending and slender spears. Great trees, holding the burdens of the storm, wait quietly for the magic touch of the warming sun, pushing its slanting rays with gentleness across the dazzling surfaces of pearl and bloom.

SIFTING SNOWS

GREAT CLOUDS of blowing sifting snows are lifted from the hills and swept by the strong northwest winds across the cold winter uplands. The turbulent masses move like swirling forms of feathered clouds over the open pastures and the fields, until the snow settles down at last in the midst of the spreading woods, or behind the farm's steep ridges, behind the fences and the walls.

Snows are whipped in blustery gales from barn roofs and evergreens, and from the meadowlands, to settle down again behind old garden hedges and in protected yards. From the shelter of his house, or from the protection of his barns, a man looks out across his hill-land acres to the turbulent movement of the snow. In the near zero gales, the sun breaks through to spread its brilliant light upon the sweeping masses left by last night's deep and quiet storm.

Swirling snows fill a man's path to his barns. His tracks are lost in the deepness of the drifts. It sifts into his barns, too, through cracks in the weathered siding and through the ventilator holes near the peak of the roof. It floats in streaming silvered strands through the slanting rays of the sun. It settles down at last upon the

19

mow, sprinkling diamonds and pearls upon timothy and clover and goldenrod.

A man will spend this day around his barns, whose great silent forms stand sturdily in the gales, breaking the force of the wind, shielding man and cow from the frigid elements. No wonder a man looks with friendly gratitude upon his barn. The century-old structure shelters and shields his team and his cows. It protects his hay and his grain. It yields a warmth in gust and in storm. And when a man returns once more to the comforts of his house, he will appreciate even more the warmth that his cows have found in the shelter of their own weathered "home," hidden from view sometimes by the great turbulent clouds of sifting snows.

SNOW ROLLERS

WINTER AFTER winter may come to a man's northeastern farm before he experiences the thrill and the delight of witnessing the rare and phenomenal snow rollers, built by the wind pushing a thin layer of thawing snow as the temperature hovers just above freezing. A countryman feels well repaid for his patience and his perseverance, for decades at a time may slip into history before the spectacle unfolds itself over the meadows of his hilly acres.

A man has observed the rollers of snow just before sunset; he has seen them shortly after sunrise. In both instances, he was especially cognizant of the fact that he could easily have missed the phenomena had the rollers, for example, been formed after dark or on a winter morning before he rose with the sun. And he knows that their stay is brief, that strong winds and dropping temperatures may soon break them up, leaving little evidence of the miracle that moved across his fields.

A countryman who has observed literally hundreds of the rollers on his uplands has every right to mark the event among the rarest and the choicest of a country winter. He is alert, naturally, to the everyday wonders of the season, the beauty of sunlight on the crisp snow, the beauty of jewels hanging from every limb and twig when the rays reach down to touch the ice-covered trees and shrubs and wires, the loveliness of a winter morning rich in frost that hangs diamonds on every object touched by the reaching fingers of the sun. But he is amazed at the spectacle of hundreds of snow rollers over his fields and meadows and pasture lands, for he has observed dozens of them, halted on the brink of a steep hill. He has known others, on reaching the crest, to go on down of their own momentum, adding more and more to their size, depending, of course, on the length of the slope. He has found, at the foot of the hill, giant wind-made rolls of snow measuring from one to two feet in diameter.

He notes that these rollers are somewhat hollowed at the ends. Thoreau wrote of their resemblance to rolls of carpet or women's muffs. A man remembers his father likening them to rolled jelly cake, with each layer of snow plainly visible. A boy once, rolling the snow into balls and building snow men, a man likes to picture the wind and the thaw as the children of winter, whistling with glee, perhaps, playing hand in hand, and building and pushing snow rollers over his meadows, and down his hills.

THE COLD WAVE

*T*HE COLD WAVE, sweeping swiftly in from the north, and enveloping a man's upland farm in a great wide belt of frigid temperature, is an expected part of winter to the northeastern countryman. Years of country living have taught him to catalogue the sudden frigid blast as a wing of the season of wind and ice and snow. They have taught him to prepare for it, and to expect it. Such a man finds beauty in the winter landscape as the cold settles down, sharply and heavily, over his pastures and fields. All afternoon he has watched the mercury drop, and it falls more quickly as the early darkness moves in.

Evening comes, and he listens to the roar of the wind through the pines and the elms in his dooryard. He hears the shutters rattle, and the house, itself, creak and strain in the sudden gusts. He hears the frost tugging at the nails in the weathered siding of his house. But these are familiar sounds, because he has learned the ways of winter. And they are good sounds to a man who likes his hill farm, the year around. They are good sounds to a man, secure in his home, who feels the comforting arms of warmth reach out in a room and surround him, quietly and affectionately, in the winter night.

A man likes these things which are so much a part of the season of cold, and he likes the expectancy that sweeps over him with the coming of dawn. And he welcomes it. The wind has gone down. Stepping out of the kitchen door, he is exhilarated by the sharpness and the keenness of the air, and pleased by the crisp clear song that his footsteps make on the crusted snow as he walks to the barn. He senses the warmth inside the barn as he goes about the morning feeding of the stock.

A man appreciates the cold wave, too, for what the daylight brings. He looks out over his snow-covered hills, brilliant in the morning sun. He hears the ice snap in the creek as it settles more closely to the water level of the stream. He hears the tree sparrows chatter among themselves as they fly down from the trees and bushes and hedges to the dooryard bird feeds. He observes the chickadees and nuthatches and woodpeckers which come for their bounty. Over the high wind-swept ridge of the farm, he sees large flocks of snow buntings which have drifted in on the crest of the cold. He hears the sharp winter call of the crow. He studies the frost designs on the panes of glass in his kitchen window.

To the countryman then, who opens his eyes and his ears, with expectancy and hope, to each new day, and season, and year, the cold wave is fringed with a frosted beauty that delights him; the dawn is filled with surprise; and it echoes with song.

VOLCANOES
OF FROZEN FOAM

A COUNTRYMAN, on intimate terms with the creek that runs its wild course through his upland farm, has reason to know its many moods, temperamental as the weather and the seasons. He knows its rapid flow turned into a torrent by the summer cloudburst over his hills, or by the heavy fall rains which drench the bare brown fields. He knows the softening mood that follows quickly in the gentle footsteps of the thaw, and the thunderous springtime song when the ice breaks and the huge crystal cakes rumble downstream with the rushing and surging current. More than that, a man knows the creek's surprises, and among them, he thinks, are the rare and beautiful volcanic peaks of frozen foam that form sometimes at the foot of the deep cascades. He has learned to watch for these volcanoes after the brief winter thaw. But even so, years at a time are likely to pass before the volcanoes are observed in all their fragile beauty of lace and foam.

More than once, though, a man who has walked the banks of the farm stream has admired these volcanic cones in the shelter of the ice-covered waterfalls. He has watched the volcanoes build sometimes to heights taller than a man. The thaw had not been long and full enough to open the stream, and the foam, accumulating under the ice at the foot of the cataract, and churned by the pressure of the current, was forced through a vent. The constant pressure and the continual freezing of the foam as it spilled over the top caused the hollow cone to rise.

A man will long remember his father's vivid description of the fragile structure. "The cone," his father said, "resembles a pyramid of the lightest and creamiest lace, folded and looped and crumpled by a weight so insignificant that one sometimes wonders whether a cone as tall as a man weighs more than a few ounces. The volcanoes seldom stand more than a couple of hours after sunrise. Wind will destroy them because they are so light, and warmer weather will quickly reduce them to a few drops of water."

A countryman, who as a boy stood with his father at the side of one of the tallest cones, remembers his awe at the fluffiness, reaching into the cold like a peaked tower above him. Even then he admired the beauty and loveliness of the frail and foamy structures pointing like lacy spires into the rich morning light. Years later, the wonders of the creek still spread their beauty in the old channel. A man knows that the upland stream will yield its charm as long as water flows, as long as winters come to seal the streams, and as long as there are brief thaws in the heart of winter hours, followed by a quiet dawn of cold.

A UNIVERSE OF STARS
—A FIELD OF SUNS

TIME TURNS with the earth, and so it shall be with these stars above the fields bathed in the sheets of snow. A man can go out and look up, as Whitman, "in perfect silence at the stars." And he sees there, in this darkness of the rushing wind, a choice arrangement of designs, in the Big Dipper, and constellations, in the Morning Star, and the Evening. Stars have a way of bending in upon the hills, and he who walks in the gentle comfort of the land, looks to these embroidered pastures in the sky.

He sees his pasture framed in the pictures of the stars. He walks past the cold stone walls, and the creek's spirals of ice, and under the bare tree limbs, stretched like delicate and intricate patterns and forms against the dark night sky. Yet, he senses underfoot, another universe of stars, a slope of blossoms, of creeping thyme and shepherd's-purse, of clover and thistle and pussytoes. He senses, underfoot, a field of suns in the daisies and the fleabane.

All these are a countryman's stars, and they will never fail to light the way in their kind summer of blossom and bloom. As surely as Auriga and Orion rise out of the hills with the wheeling skies, these pasture stars will rise out of the spring of earth, the stitchwort and elecampane and mullein. The snows swirl in on the wings of the wind, but they will never cover these endless dreams.

A man has winter at his finger tips in the spinning stars of cold. But he also has his summer of dreams, and his spring of hopes, the warming of the ageless earth in the never-ending pulse of pasture lands. He looks up at the distant stars; he hears the hum of a gentle wind through the meadow grass; he sees the stars of blossoms moving in the breeze upon a hill. He smells the delicate and rich perfume of the wild evening primrose though winter has folded the brittle forms under the crust of snow. These blossoms of meadow and field and pasture are a man's stars, as truly as the brilliant forms that step out into the darkness to twinkle and gleam in the pastures of the sky.

A WOOD ROAD THAT WINDS UP A HILL

T HE WINTER wood road, reaching its inquisitive way through the oak and the beech and the maple, and on between the groves of snow-draped hemlocks, can be as palatial to a countryman as the quiet room in which royalty is crowned, or as rich and full of inspiration as the vast cathedrals in their settings of beauty and devout dignity. The charm and the inspiration of the winter wood road may be found in the new morning's light on a zero day, or in the mellowing glow of an afternoon, for there is peace here, and there is humble quiet. This is the greatest cathedral a man has known, built by the centuries of a spinning universe.

One who faces the strong biting gales and the swirling snows through the wind-swept pastures and open fields to his woods, anticipates the peaceful comfort that awaits him deep in a forest that is home for the deer and the rabbit and the squirrel. It is home for the nuthatch and the chickadee and the grouse. The songs and chords he hears are played on organs far older than those which yield soft music from those structures which are built by man. The winter chords have a melody that has resounded through wheeling ages of suns and glistening stars.

Here, there is the music of wind playing on the harps of the land. There is something permanent about the chords that have kept on coming through the years. Yet there is the vigor and the zest of youth in the force of the strong fresh gales. There is serenity of age in the more gentle winds. The chord is a rhythmic one, reaching time and again from a sharp whistling crescendo all the way down to a whisper of content. It reaches from some vast thundering power to a lullaby as soft as a newly fallen snow, or as the woodland moss.

This is an old woods, and it harbors old trees. No doubt generations of squirrels and chickadees and deer have found their way into its quietness. Under the oaks, squirrels have dug down through the snow for their acorns, hidden in the warm leaf-mold of the forest floor. A deer has followed the path to the gurgling stream. A chickadee calls. This may be the song of something young, but it belongs forever in the atmosphere of content that one so surely finds as he climbs the carpeted stairway of his farm—a wood road that winds up a hill.

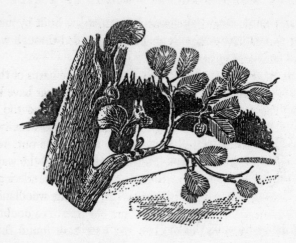

WINTER HARVEST

THE TRUE countryman sees far more in his winter days than the brown earth or the white fields over which he walks. There is far more to him, in winter, than the spears of zero days and biting winds, and far more than the crunching of snow underfoot. The true countryman has grown up with the seasons; he has faced the snowstorms, and the walls of steel-like cold from the beginning of the season, to the end, and for year upon year. He knows that a winter has endless possibilities for thought and understanding, no matter where his steps may take him.

To many, perhaps, the idea of the harvest is one that goes with the full fall fields, and the ripened crops stored in a man's barns. Winter, too, has a harvest, one that is rich and memorable. And a countryman gathers it thoughtfully. Nor does he have to go far afield. On the hills of his rolling farm, the harvest awaits him, though his may be quiet fields, under the heavy blankets of snow.

When a man goes out through the pasture bars, and across the icy slopes, his harvest unfolds before him in all that comes in view of his eyes, or within sound of his ears. Where the brown blades of last year's grass and weeds pierce the crusted surface of the snow, a swirl of tree sparrows and goldfinches settles down at a winter table. The clusters of seeds held by the brittle stalks and the dried stems have not surrendered their richness to the icy draughts of wind and cold.

The pines spread out in a grove of green before him. He hears the wind, playing on the harp-like strings of their branches and their boughs. This is a harvest of song that is as ageless as the centuries. There is the song of the winter creek as the water bubbles unseen below the ice; it throbs like a summer vein close to the arms of the hills. The creek has found its own in a shielding armor of silver and white.

The man who walks this way reaches on to his highest hill, and he looks back across the rolling meadows and over the steep slopes to the wild pasture, back across the land to a house that stands in quietness in the valley, out of the wind. All through his fields, a man finds a harvest of dreams, one that is never done, even under the tilted plates and the hardened hoods of drifts. It is the grain of growth awaiting a man in the heart of the hills. There will come a time when the earth swings, in a softer vein, toward spring. A new song and sun will break in waves across the sea of grass and over the ledges. This is a harvest, lying dormant now; a patient crop of seeds awaiting the warming keys of the sun.

A PICKETED WALL
AND DRIFTING SNOW

A STONE WALL, with a row of pickets built across its top to keep the hens from flying over from the farmyard into the garden, can yield a winter beauty almost unparalleled in this season of snow and cold.

One almost thinks of the snow and the wind and the fence as the children of winter, playing their own and respective roles in building the deep and scalloped drifts along the sheltered walls.

Yet, when the playing is done, the art is of such intricacy and loveliness that one must surely think the season is like a weathered man of the hills. In spite of an outward callousness, there is song within the heart.

So it is with man who may complain, or speak disparagingly, of the long weeks of cold. Deep within himself, he cannot help but see the beauty of a snow-covered field. All of the outdoor year is his, even in those days when he must plod through knee-deep snows to his hillside woods.

The sun will come eventually, after storms. Spring will come, too. Each of the seasons has its richer and its better phase. After the winter storm, it could well be the sun, pouring a brilliant light over the hills and woods. It could well be the sun tracing the shadows of trees and their branches and limbs in sprawling and almost complex figures over the crusted drifts. It is as though the snow were a mirror, reflecting the images of the reaching branches of the hickory and the apple and the elm.

Winter has a charming way of building these scalloped and hardened drifts along the old wall fence that follows a row of lilacs by the lane from the shelter of the barn to the muffled song of the stream. These drifts, bathed in winter's brilliant sun, sparkle with gems and with jewels. It is a winter bloom that must surely pass, in time, just as the lilacs, towering above the fence, will yield their rich May blossoms to the quiet green of a summer leaf. Each has its season. Each has its hour, like the glistening sunrise at dawn or the mellow and golden glow that precedes a serene sunset across the hills.

A man has seen farm boys wear their winter caps with their peaked tops, a sort of igloo shape except the tops were more pointed and sharp than they were round. He has found the same peaked features built up from the banks of snow along the wall.

He has found the shadows of the spreading branches, reaching out and over the deep cold drifts, tracing a way of contentment, perhaps, from winter's snow to the comforting shade of the summer leaf and bough.

ALDER BERRIES
IN SNOW

THE BERRY of the black alder, a northeastern countryman thinks, may well deserve the same important place in a man's farm as does the berry of the holly on some wide spreading plantation under a southern sun. A man who has seen both the holly and the alder, and who has long been familiar with their vivid winter charm, wishes the alder might always play its brilliant role in a world of northern snow, just as the holly adds richness to the softer southern winter.

A northern countryman knows his frequent winter walks to the alder swamps will yield bright hues of red and scarlet. He sees the panoramic glow spread quietly against the brown carpet of the bogs, when there have been unseasonal rains to bare the hills. He sees the colors flame against the deep still mass of white, when there have been storms to dump great layers of snow across cold hills and valley lands.

A man has found the rich red color of the alder berries casting

35

a vivid hue in an hour of falling snow. Such a man likes to have black alder swamps to beckon him on through the long slow chill of a season that seems in no hurry at all to unravel or loosen its taut sharp strings.

A man feels that he would be in a strange world, indeed, if the hills did not have their swamps and bogs. And just as a countryman will pull his overcoat together against the winter wind, he likes to think the scarlet berries of the black alder are tiny beads, buttoned snugly and warmly against the snowy vest of the land.

A GIRL, A CHICKADEE, AND MAN

I<small>T NEED</small> not be a smile that a man sees on the face of a little girl when the blackcapped chickadee flies down from the spreading branches of the elm, or from the veranda columns, to feed from her outstretched hand.

And, for that matter, maybe the girl is somewhat afraid to accept the impulse that would have her smile, afraid that even the movement of her soft smooth cheeks would frighten away this warm and curious bundle of friendship that she had so suddenly found.

The richest winter hour may well have been that quiet morning of sun and cold when a wondering child, filled with confidence, held out her hand on which she had placed the crumbled scraps of doughnuts, and the broken meats of the hickory nut and the butternut. Standing close to the veranda column in the sheltered corner of the porch, a girl saw a chickadee bring hope to her dreams.

She had found the miracle of the tender touch of a bird's toes, clinging to a finger, transmitting something beyond words and description, when the chickadee, at last, cast out its fears and started to dine from the palm of her opened hand. No wonder the gleaming lines of satisfaction were written so richly, and yet so quietly, across the face of the child.

Spring has started to push in on the closing gates of winter, and one can look back with the same kind of satisfaction upon the weeks of a season that is ebbing now. Memories can be as warm as the rays of a climbing sun, starting to lift the cold and to melt the snow, starting to pull the frost out of the hard and frozen soil. Memories can be etched in the sun of content for one who has spent weeks, feeding the birds, which came in flocks over his snow-covered dooryard and his gardens.

Bird feeding, a countryman says, pays the richest kind of dividends in this winter phase of country living. A man can make it as natural a part of the season as chore-time, and woodcutting. It can spread contentment through the long hours of snow. It can yield a touch of warmth to winter's frigidness. It can yield a bit of song, soft and tender and good, a song unlike the whistling of the sharp winter wind that sweeps down from the hills.

When the snows lie heavy on the land, a man's walks are likely to be more abbreviated than those when the meadows found softness in the summer sun. Breaking a path through the deep and crusted surface that blankets the slopes is not as easy as a rambling walk through the open fields.

So a man is more inclined to let some of the season come in to his door. He invites as much of it as he can by providing rations for the chickadees and nuthatches and woodpeckers, and for the tree sparrows. And when they will come, there are rations, too, for the goldfinch and the purple finch, and even for the wintering song sparrow which moves in from the brush thicket along a quiet slope facing the winter sun.

Snow buntings will move in, too, now and then, leaving to the cold and the sweeping gales the higher ridges of a rolling farm. A meadowlark, wintering in the neighborhood, may well wing its way over the garden to the bordering meadow, where the dried crowns of the goldenrod and the wild carrot and the timothy are held above the snow. Nor does a man have the heart to drive the blue jay from his door.

Winter after winter, the birds come back. He knows that many generations of them have found the shelter of his quiet house as kind as that of a deep and sheltered valley by a woodland stream. He knows that birds and their songs have a way of shortening these hours that otherwise would step with a vexing slowness from one day to another. He listens to a constant chattering, expressing perhaps, in a bird's way, something of contented gratitude.

He is a man of wisdom who lets the chickadee and the tree sparrow, the nuthatch and the woodpecker, draw the cheerlessness out of the winter hour, and put in its stead the round and feathered bundles of warmth, the movement of wings, the song of content from the sweeping limbs of the pine and the elm and the maple.

Birds are a man's winter neighbors. They will come as surely as the light and the sun.

CANDLES OF THE HILLS

*T*HE OSIER and the willow are like the wands of the season, holding proudly their glowing spires of red and gold in a winter hour. It would surely seem that their roots must reach far into the warmth of the earth where the fingers of spring have a tender way of transmitting the softening touch of the year long before the northern hills and streams are opened by the sun.

Day by day, the osier and the willow show the effects, more and more, of the approaching March sun, or the spring rain. The red of the osier brightens almost into flame. The willow turns more golden. One detects a glow against the deep and crusted blanket of the snow.

A man rather expects that the chickadees and the tree sparrows could warm their toes on the twigs and branches, soft with earth and with sun. He expects the muskrat, moving with rippled ease in the swamp's channel through the osier-bordered bogs, must certainly find the water a little warmer where the reddened spires point upward through the snow. Spring, working through the deep seams of the earth and the hills, is far ahead of the bluebird and the bloom.

Perhaps, a countryman says, the lowlands are a little closer to the pulse of the throbbing veins below the frostline, under the ice and under the snow. He likes to think the osier and the willow are the conductors through which the breathing warmth of earth reaches ever up into the cold. They are the wicks on the candles of the hills, lighting the hallway of the year so that winter can step more surely into spring.

KEY TO A
WINTER WOODS

*E*VERY TIME a countryman walks out across the railroad swamp,
and up the long steep hill to the growth of hemlocks on a high summit overlooking his house, he likes to think that the pileated woodpecker has left a key to the woods on the trunk of an old tree on the
forest's edge. Great triangular gashes where the woodpecker has
worked show up distinctly in the afternoon light of the winter sun.
A man accepts the key. He enters the forest as the silence and the
rigidity of the winter's day close in more tightly upon the hemlocks.

Once in the woods, a man perceives the magnificence of trees
all around him. He walks among them. Their friendly forms reach
high into the wind in a cold sky. Deep in the woods, he feels no
wind, though the gales push on in roaring strength overhead. This
is a quiet walk among the hemlocks, and he is comforted by trees.
The atmosphere, of course, is in sharp contrast with that which he
found as he worked his way up the steep slopes.

Down on the frozen swamp, the dried and brittle cattails rose up
from the ice like the hard teeth of a brush; they rustled in the icy
sweep of the wind. In the open pasture, the wind pushed at his
face and his hands. Here there is no wind, though high above, there
is movement and uneasiness among the tops of the tall trees. There
is movement, too, as the pileated woodpecker dips and rises in its
flight through the winter air.

A man walks and dreams. The sun has slipped lower toward the
rim of the western slopes. And when he leaves the woods, he can

look down upon a valley of houses and trees and a frozen swamp reaching like an arm along the foot of the slope. He scans the sweep of the valley. And from his vantage point, on the summit of the hill, the old farm structures below look like houses in a toy-land. They seem small and unreal. The valley trees point to the sky like long and fragile wires, bending in a wind. Even the shadows are thin as they spread out across the snow.

A countryman feels that he stands on the threshold to a dreamland. A walk into the height of his hills has pushed the houses in the valley out of their greatness into miniature things. Here is a watcher of the setting sun, looking out over the spreading acres of his upland farm and the acres of his neighbors, looking down upon the old farm structures, growing more tiny and inconspicuous in a winter's twilight. Woods and the open snow-covered fields spread a patchwork of dark and white into the doorway of the night. A man rests his hand against the friendly trunk of an ancient hemlock in the edge of the forest. Splinters and the workings of the pileated woodpecker are scattered at the foot of the tree, and the chiseled figure on the trunk where the bird has probed hangs like a strange key upon the gleaming door of a winter woods.

VIBRANT SYMPHONY

A MAN, RELAXED and warm in the comforts of his house, rather likes a winter's night of wind, pouring out in rolling chords over the hills while the moon spreads its soft flowing light through the broken and swift-moving clouds. And where the skies are clear and cold, stars add a sparkling delight to the wind's mischievous ways. One may well think of the gusts and gales as capricious children of the season, racing with glee across the fields, and playing in the woods.

The wind came quickly and with strength long before the sun went down. It scampered around the house, playing tag with snow-flakes, and with fallen autumn leaves which once had found shelter behind the hedges and the walls. It glided swiftly over roofs and through the spires of bending trees. It played with the smoke, rising uneasily from the chimneys on a house.

The wind was vibrant, and almost tireless in its steady sweep across the land. It pushed at the downy feathers of a bird, and sent the crows sailing through the afternoon sky. It whipped at the fur of the kitten and the squirrel. It swept briskly like a broom through the dried and browned reeds in the swamp. It pushed at the cones of the pine, and sent them skating over ice, and on the crusts of snow.

The vigor of the season poured out in strong and swirling chords. The wind whistled and hummed and roared. It rattled the ancient blinds and the loose windowpanes. It twisted and swayed the branches of the dooryard elms and the boughs of the roadside pines. And when a man at last closed his eyes for his night of rest, he could picture the broken clouds racing through the sky. The wind played on. It would fade, and then pick up again. A chord that seemed lost in the night would rebound once more from the upland ridge. And a man listened long to this vibrant symphony from the hills.

WHIRLPOOLS AND ICE

SOMETIMES, AFTER the farm creeks have opened to the rain and the sun and the thaw, and the thundering cargoes of ice have, for the most part, pounded their way wildly through the turbulent gorge between the hills, there may come a more placid hour in the current of the flow.

The weather, likely as not, dips again with its winter-like hands into the colder basins of the freezing temperatures and the driving winds. The pressure from the hills has gone with the thaw. The water recedes, and a man will start his search for the whirling discs of ice, spinning like saucers in the whirlpools of the stream.

The search may come on a day after a wet spring-like snow has moved in softly to cover the hills once more. It may have spread its white deep blankets down to the shore lines of the creek. The snow may even cover the great cakes of ice that have lodged against the rocks and ledges. It may cover the ice that had been halted on its swift strong ride on the swollen current of the stream.

A man can always walk along the shores of the creek that has followed its course for the centuries through the hills and woods and pastures of his rolling farm.

He can walk for the creek's song, the year around. He knows well its muffled winter chords, followed by the wild spring chorus. He is familiar with the trickling summer brook, and the clear and bell-

45

like notes of the liquid flow. He knows the heavier splashing melody played by the drumming fingers of the persistent autumn rains.

He can walk for its beauty, for the silver of winter ice, and the loveliness of snow clinging to the sloping banks and cliffs. There is, in turn, the good freshness of the swift spring freshet when the splashing waters stir up great mounds of foam, reaching up from the turbulent cascades to be whipped away in the wind. There is the rich and cooling comfort of a summer hour; then the autumnal brilliance when the red and the orange and the gold of the coloring leaves spread their own bright images in the clear and quiet pools.

Through all his seasons, a man has found beauty in the upland stream, reaching all the way from the towering castles of silvered ice built by winter and the plunging waterfalls, to the summer arch of shade, spread across the gorge by the branches of the birch and the basswood and the maple.

Yet late winter and spring have revealed some of the most artistic work of the moving fingers of the tender and softening year. Far down from a waterfall somewhere, where the current had found its more gradual level again, and seemed in less of a hurry to plunge its way through the valley, he has found a cake of ice, round as a disc, spinning in the swirling current, spinning around and around like a platter on the surface of the pool.

He may well suspect that the ice had been trapped in a whirlpool, held in its place by the swirling current and by the large chunks of ice downstream, or by protruding rocks reaching up from the bed of the creek. He sort of imagines the disc had been formed by the constant and even wearing of the swirling current and by bumping constantly into the rocks and ice that held it in the pool. It becomes more and more circular, spinning on and on as a top will spin.

The time may come when rising waters will move the whirling disc down through the gorge with the surging flow again, pounding it to fragments, perhaps, over the rocks and ledges and waterfalls.

Or else the climbing sun may push its kind and warming rays deeper and deeper into the spinning disc, reducing it to a porous shell, to be lost, at last, forever to the ages.

GROUND PINE
AND HEMLOCK

THE GREEN of the pine and the hemlock and spruce, spreading
their darkened spires across a man's uplands, is not the only green
to be found in his winter hills. By a wooded path, the great broad
leaves of the rhododendron rest on the deep rippled carpet of snow.
The steep woodland bank by the creek is lush with juniper. Leaves
of the partridge berry vine and the wintergreen are hidden among
the fallen feathered flakes, out of the way of ice and wind. And in
the quiet and frosted realm of a forest, a man finds green spools and
twists of the ground pine, weaving in and out of the snow and the
softening leaves. Its clusters, which twine on the avenues of the
leaves, are witnesses to the changing sky of trees and limbs above.
Yet it holds its green on a loom of frozen flakes and silvered ice
under the bright sparkling points of a million stars when the year
brings its inevitable change to the slopes.

When the snows are deep, and the winds sweep wildly across the
summits of the land, a countryman can stroll over the frozen earth

of the forest, and press with his walking stick through the broad overcoat worn by the hills. To his satisfaction and delight, he discovers the fan-shaped ground pine resting under its shield of white. He brings it to light by his curiosity; a summer-like green unfurls before his eyes.

It is a green that contrasts vividly with the brown leaves around it, and with the white of the snow. It is secure in a man's woods, where it holds its treasures against the reaching arms of the seasons, the alternating fingers of cold and heat that push down over the rugged and rocky land.

A man knows well the sharpness and strength of the season, and the close ties of the ice and the storm with the sunlight and the shadow that have walked these acres. Here is a green that steps quietly through all the year. The hidden veins reach on and on under the rich white blankets that cover the wooded floor. A man knows that when spring comes again, racing in with bluebird songs and waving hepatica blooms, and a fresh new hue finds its way to field and pasture land, he will find in his woods a green that has persisted through the long cold days and nights. The ground pine holds its lines well. It seems eternal. It seems content in a man's woods, whether it lies under a winter's covering, or whether it builds a carpet of loveliness over the floor of a world which the squirrels and the deer claim for their upland meadow and home.

MARCH SNOW

ANYONE WHO has for years watched the return of March to the uplands, still does not know just what to expect of the hours. He never knows for sure whether the days will be mild enough to start arousing the hepatica and the arbutus, or whether the month will be one of storms and flurries and squalls, storms that often bring the deepest and heaviest snows of the winter.

A countryman who has known March in all its moods has seen the tender days come early, releasing the hills of their snow, opening the bogs, and thawing the hyla into song. But he has seen, too, the heavy snows cover his rolling acres and his roads. He has seen these storms, late in the month, force him to walk three miles to the post office, just as other generations had done in those days when there were no such conveniences as rural free delivery and good paved roads by the door.

The storm that swirls in just ahead of April must give way, of course, to the sun and the thaw. April will surely coax spring back again. The March snow, though it tells a man to take up his shovel, to clear paths and driveways and walks, and to free the roofs strained by the snow's wet heaviness, yields what he thinks is something special in the way of song. Here is a composition as old as the hills, blending the sharper winter chords into the softer melodies of spring.

Robins and bluebirds, which had already made their singing return to the northern hills, flock about the dooryard elms and maples, and the hedges in the garden. The song sparrow sends out an old and delightful trill from the bending branches of the forsythia, only a few short weeks away from its golden canopy of bloom. The fox sparrow moves in from the pasture thicket to spread a vivid and rusty red against the white of a country dooryard. The red-winged blackbirds stay close to the clumps of alders and pussy willows that fringe the low-lying border of a farm meadow. The killdeer plover calls from a pasture under snow. The winter birds come back, too, to the dooryard feeds. And the junco comes, and the purple finch feeds from the dried seed clusters of the mountain ash by the door. Out in the meadows, where the browned stalks of weeds hold their brittle crowns above the snow, the buntings swirl and dive in rhythmic unison with the frigid blasts of wind sweeping swiftly out of the north.

More than once the late March snows have sent nearly a hundred birds to feed and chirp and sing about the dooryard trees and feeding shelves. In less than an hour, on such a day, a man has counted, in the immediate vicinity of his house, more than twenty species of birds, seeking sustenance and quiet shelter from the hands of the provident countryman. The warming earth of spring, even now, works at the blanket of snow from underneath. And from overhead, there comes a medley of songs to offer a carol for the swollen buds, shielded by the quiet covering of snow. The March storm brings a rich snow, indeed. It is one through which the soft fingers of the year push with vibrant tenderness, while winter still adds its delectable tart to the first spring hours.

SPRING IN A SWAMP

*L*ONG BEFORE the hepatica would dare to push its smiling blossoms out of the steaming leaf-mold in the softening carpet of the woods, a countryman, anxious for the first spring blooms, will surely go out to the swamps and the lowlands of his upland farm. It is there that the pussy willow and the alder cling with proud persistence to the rim of the water-filled basins of his woods and fields.

The catkins start to open, days and even weeks ahead of the season's tender and charming bow across the threshold of a man's rolling acres. Spring need not have taken the ice from the rippled current of the stream, winding slowly through the cattails and the reeds in the old channel. Spring need not have taken the snow from the hills. Each year, a man has found the opened catkins in days when the snow lay with heaviness upon the land, and when the bogs, which harbor the skunk cabbage, were still at rest under the quietness of winter's deep blanket of white.

He has found the catkins of the pussy willow bursting forth from their small red jackets in a day when the winds were sharp with the arrows of cold from some polar region. A man thought they seemed in something of a hurry to throw off their coats to the spring sun and a warming rain. He has found the blossoms, glistening in the brilliance of the late winter sun, sparkling almost, like drops of water from the swollen buds of the maple and the elm and the lilac, hung like a strand of beads upon a neck of the hills. These, a countryman likes to think, are the pearls of spring, trembling in the wind, moving with a pulsatory rhythm that makes them rise and fall with the breathing slopes of the land.

The catkins of the pussy willow will keep on opening until they reach a fluffy cotton-like softness. The reddish brown catkins of the alder hang downward from the twigs, like tiny fingers from a hand, relaxed and warm. For the first spring blossoms, a man will be sure to go out to his hill-land swamp, resounding with the flute-like notes of the red-winged blackbirds which spark the thickets with the flaming red of their sweeping wings. With such warmth of color, and with such softness of bloom, it is not hard to understand why the spring sun will, in time, rouse the sleeping hyla from its dreams.

WHEN HILLS
RELAX AGAIN

MARCH ALWAYS brings spring to a man's door. Dooryard ways are more gentle now. The hills, too, relax, and a countryman walks into them for a broader sweep of sun and liquid songs and softening fields. The open fields are already free of snow as if the rollicking strain of the robin had done its part to draw the frigidness from the land. In the shadow of the wood lot, though, and in the shade of stone walls and thickets, curving and thinning banks of snow still hold their conspicuous forms in the deepening warmth. But even the wasting drifts, once fresh and new in the strength of winter days, seem far less cold than they did before winter withdrew to make way once more for the swinging season of bud and song.

The uplands are mild in these warming days. The slopes steam in the sun, and though they yet may feel the sudden driving squalls of snow, the earth is already at work with this season of spring. Swollen buds push leaves aside, and the grass starts to spread its

53

carpet of green across the land. Countless events are taking place in these very hills as spring moves in where winter walked with cold and icy step. A man recalls Thoreau's remark that he "had no idea there was so much going on in Heyward's meadow."

Meanwhile, in the shade of the pines and the old walls, white shields of snow shine in the March sun. From a distance, the drifts seem to hang strangely, like blades of white upon the aprons of the fields. Coming more closely, however, one stands on the fringe of the moisture-filled mounds, snow that has turned to brownish hues from the dust and the seeds it has caught from a hurried winter's wind. The drifts are softening. The snow melts, sending miniature streams of water into the receptive earth. Some of it is sent on down the hills by the quick and penetrating thaw.

A countryman sees here, in these thinning drifts of snow, something of a winter's postscript, a lingering message from the heart of a season when winds and snows whipped across the frozen fields. And yet, with the warble of the bluebird in the air, and swelling hepatica buds pushing through the leaf carpet in the woods, a countryman finds little to remember of any discontent of frigid zero days. Winter has never been too long once a man hears the trill of a song sparrow from a thicket or a hedge.

AN EAR FOR SONG

Spring never comes too soon for a man who is friend to the maples and the hills. For weeks he has been building and planning, but he would have it so. The sun and the softening hours have played hand in hand upon his wishes and his dreams. He knows the hour must come when the sun will mould its warmth into the contours of the land, and the mercury will climb, and the sap will rise again in the old maples. These days herald a rich sweet maple flow; they herald the songs and the carols of birds winging their way north once more from a southern winter. These days remind a man of the first spring that he can remember.

The sun smiles down upon the hills, after a sharp crisp night to start the sap dripping from the spiles. A man hears the song of the first bluebird carried on the wings of the morning from an old apple orchard on the hill. He watches the melting snow work and turn into miniature streams down the paths and roads. Day draws to a close, and he is delighted by the richness and the color of the first robin, facing the west and the afternoon sun, issuing an old spring carol from the topmost branch of the dooryard elm. It is the same elm from which a robin sang in that first remembered spring. A man remembers an old sap house, built out of stone in the edge of the woods, facing the south and east. Only the tumbled stones remain, yet there are still the same clear nights in the March woods, hours in the moonlight, and wood-fire smoke working its way surely and steadily into the sharp night air.

Every man, a countryman thinks, should have an ear for song, so that he will miss none of the delight when spring and maple-tapping time step in over the crest of the hill. One after another the spring songs issue from the throats of birds moving through the softening skies over an upland farm.

FROM ROSTRUMS
OF RIPPLED HALLS

THERE ARE springs when a countryman finds himself waiting night after night for the shrill and piping voice of the first hyla. He has known a north country March to turn to a steady warmth that seemed to tug at the very depths of the bogs, rousing the spring peepers into song. On the other hand, a man has gone all the way through March before the clear shrill medley rang out in all its bell-like vigor from swamps and farm ponds.

When the hyla is early in giving its piping answer to the old spring urge, a countryman finds the shrill notes, coming slowly and feebly at first, with only a few scattered voices from here and there among the reeds and cattails. The din of the medley increases with the progress of the season, growing richer as the warmth becomes deeper and more sure. The early springs, though, are often halted, briefly at least, by the sudden cold that tumbles the temperatures below freezing again. These biting nights bring as sudden an end to the swampland chorus. At best, perhaps, a man will hear a few piping calls, alone and slow and far apart.

But if the peeper should wait for April to rouse the chorus, a man can surely hope for a constant burst of song, coming with a well-established vigor and a certainty. This is the kind of spring that fills the first night of April song into a rapturous melody, as though the peepers had waited for this very hour to lift the curtain on the rostrum of their rippled halls.

Hylas must be more patient than man, a countryman thinks, when they leave the balconies of the hills in a silence more deep than the darkness that enfolds them. Peepers must be patient, indeed, to retain a quietness through all the cold expectant weeks of spring, until the warmth is so sure that every bog resounds with a rhythmic sweep of song undulating through the April hours.

SONG FROM THE STARS

ALL OF the delights of spring, a countryman knows, cannot always be found at a man's finger tips. The robin and the bluebird and the song sparrow will come to a man's dooryard, the swallow and phoebe to his sheds and his barns, the flicker to the roadside maples, and the meadowlark to his fields. But if a man wants to add to his enjoyment of the season, the rich sweet flight-song of the woodcock, he must go to his wooded swamps or his marshland thickets. And he must go with patience in his heart, for nights at a time may pass before the old treasure unfolds again on a warm spring evening.

A man who has heard the woodcock in his skyward ascent is more than reluctant to let a single spring go by without a trip to the swamp to listen to the rich and jubilant carol. Or he may hear the "peent"-like voice of this nocturnal bird. A man has gone to the marsh each spring; he has waited for dusk, and the woodcock's song. And he has heard that song, spring after spring, woven into the dew-filled hour that follows the brilliance of a setting sun.

The spiraling flight of the bird, a man thinks, is something to behold. A man faces the west, so that the silhouette of the bird in its flight can be more easily observed against the glow of the evening sky. Upward and upward the woodcock climbs, issuing its call from the deepening darkness. Then, suddenly, with a swift plunge, the bird returns to earth. A man has known the bird, after its descent, to come up so closely to him that, had he dared to extend an arm, he could have touched a wing. A man would wait for hours; he would wait for springs, even, for the flight-song of the woodcock, issued so richly and joyously from a sphere of the stars.

GENTLE AS WINGS
OF A BUTTERFLY

ALONG ABOUT the time of year when rhubarb leaves in a countryman's garden are the size of saucers or small plates, a soft canopy
of bloom moves in over the dooryard when the elms come quietly
into flower. It yields an illuminating hue of brown to the whole
atmosphere of the great and undulating spread of the giant trees.
Spring surely must tug at the heartstrings of the elm, just as it tugs
at those of a man.

From one of the lowest-hanging limbs, drooping within reach of
man, a countryman has before him a bouquet of flowers, minutely
feathery, and soft and tender as the down of the nestling bird. The
blossoms are exquisitely beautiful, a man thinks, but the fragile and
intricate loveliness may well go unseen and unobserved.

Winds move the blossoms with the swaying limbs in the April
sun. Showers touch them with a refreshing softness. With such
tempting warmth as April can yield, it is little wonder that the

green pushes up from the hills. It is little wonder that the wake-robin blooms.

A countryman finds it difficult, indeed, to perceive all of the colors that a single cluster of elm blossoms yields, and when wing after wing of the feathery blooms unfurls on the tips of the bending boughs, he finds a conglomeration of hues, the tenderest of tints, symbolic of spring. There is none of the brilliance nor the vigor of color that sweeps across the land with the autumn frosts and sun.

Here are blossoms, held by the faintly green stems, moving more softly than the wings of a butterfly. There is a mixture of faint pinks and maroons, purples and dainty greens, swaying in a wind so gentle that it can hardly be felt by man. A countryman wonders how anything as old and sturdy and strong as the giant dooryard elm can unfurl such fragile loveliness. He is almost tempted to compare the ancient elm to a man of hills, for April after April brings softness to his weathered face, transforming its features of strength into a smiling countenance.

FENCE MENDING TIME

*E*VERY MAN knows that good fences are symbols of good husbandry. Few would dare to think of letting a spring go by without mending those fences that hem in their steep hill pasture lands. The pasturing season means that fences must be strong and secure, and so a man is likely to take the early spring days after the frost has gone from the ground, to rebuild and to make repairs.

Spring, here in the north, on the borderline of the year that brings nights of frost and days of thaw, frequently causes the ground to heave. Fence posts are often pushed from the ground. They must be driven in firmly again. Other posts have been broken, and they must be replaced. Old and broken wire, too, must be mended or replaced. Huge drifts of snow in winter sometimes break the wires as well as the old and aging posts.

The old stone wall needs attention too. Some of the boulders and stones have been toppled from the fence by the heaving ground. Woodchucks, which burrow under the foundations, sometimes cause the walls to tumble. These must be laid up again.

A man looks forward to fence mending time. It is, perhaps, the first farm work that takes him afield where the grass is turning green, where pasture streams send a silvered flow down the old spring hills. Beyond the fence that follows through a corner of the woodlot, hepaticas are coming into bloom, the trillium nods in the sun, and the anemone blooms in the thin sloping woods.

There may be clouds and spring showers; the wind may be damp and cool, but the song sparrow sings and the grouse drums in the woods. On those days after a soft sprinkling of snow has been spilled upon the land, the rich liquid song of the fox sparrow may be heard from the pasture ledge.

Likely as not, before the day ends, the weather will clear, and the spring sun will spread its soft light across the warming meadows and the hills. A man likes to think of fence mending time as the connecting link between the spring-soaked fields and the firmer ground of a season that is well established and strong, when cows may graze again in the sun-warmed pasture lands.

THE SOIL
AWAITS THE SEED

*I*T IS GOOD for a man to get back again on the mellowing land in the spring of the year. Thaws and warming rains have long since lifted the frost from the ground. The sun has prepared the earth for the plow and the harrow. The soil is ready for the seed. And the great hours of preparation have long been under way, longer even than the time since the soft evening when the hylas tuned up in the swamps and the bogs, tuned up slowly like a great orchestra, testing their flutes and reeds and chords. And then, in one swift sweep of surging rhythm, when April lifted the baton, the entire orchestra joined in with the bursting spring processional, loud and persistent and clear, yet delightful and mild.

Spring work on the land brings the good clean aroma of the fresh loam, the smell of earth. It brings the new spring furrow behind the plow. It brings the song of the harrow, turning and mixing the soil and stone across the fields. A man is glad now, perhaps, that he has been "old-fashioned" enough to keep the traditional farm team on his upland acres. He likes to walk behind the plow and the harrow. He likes the sounds. It makes his work easier, he thinks, to walk and move with the chords and carols of birds across the hills.

A countryman likes to get his feet on the ground. It brings him, he thinks, close to the very heartbeat of the land, close to the hills' pulse, throbbing with spring, warm and receptive with life. A man prepares his land for the grain; his garden for the seed. Every step and every movement is one of hope, brought to a rich crescendo by each returning spring of bud and blossom and leaf.

DOORYARD FORSYTHIA

THE FORSYTHIA, a man thinks, should always have a place in hedges and dooryards and country gardens. Its blossoms have a way of softening spring's sunless days of clouds and dampness and rain. Or, in the dazzling light of the clear, bright hours, the gold seems even deeper and more brilliant, as if the flowers themselves were miniature mirrors, reflecting something of the warmth and the glow of the kind spring sun.

A man will pause often to take in the beauty by his doorstep as he enters the house, and again as he leaves. He will take to himself all that he can of the yellow blooms, glistening in the new fresh light of day. He will take to himself all that he can of their noon-time hue and quietness, and all that he can of their more serene touch in the maturing afternoon. All will have their hour in an April day.

The forsythia means even more to a man who knows the role that the shrub will play in a summer song. The leafy branches are sure to hold the nest of the summer chippy, or a song sparrow's home. Here, by a kitchen door, a man harbors, almost affectionately, a glowing bush which, some day soon, will shelter and shield the house of a bird. He knows there will be melodies in a summer dawn. The melody will be as sure and rich and sweet as the forsythia itself is rich in flowering loveliness.

A countryman wants each spring that comes to turn into a golden brilliance the quiet corner by his farm doorstep, just as the pale yellow blossoms of the fly honeysuckle must surely brighten the door of the rabbit's woodland home. A man has found the forsythia lighting the paths to the doors of upland homes year after year. And on his spring day walks, he has startled many a rabbit from its bed of sleep under a canopy of honeysuckle blooms.

APPLE BLOSSOM TIME

A MAN FINDS a beauty unexcelled when apple blossoms scatter their color and aroma among the friendly trees, holding graciously their uncontested place in the sun, across orchards and pastures. It is little wonder that a man likes to stand back to get a perspective of his sprawling hillsides, the orchards, the wild trees that have come up in the thin pastures, and along stone walls.

This is the spring harvest among the apple blossoms. The bees, with a satisfied hum, one that even sounds like contentment, go about their work of gathering the nectar. Not until the clover blossoms, a man thinks, will the bees find another such yield.

Nothing pleases a countryman more than his sidehills of apple trees when the season of bloom writes its ever-recurring lines in beauty and song across the slopes. Bluebirds warble richly from the branches near their sheltered house. A robin scolds, though needlessly, because a man walks too closely to the strawberry apple tree where she has her nest; the leaves will soon hide her home among the boughs.

A man will be sure, if he can, to be near his trees when a gentle wind, or a rain, starts the showers of soft petals floating to the ground. Before that hour, the orchard leaves nothing unsaid to a man; quietly she opens her heart through the spreading blooms; the bees keep humming. And the hills wear a floral garland in the quiet dignity that befits their majestic acceptance of the marching centuries.

FROM BLOSSOM
TO LEAF

*I*T IS A new kind of spring that greets the countryman in May; the hesitancy and indecision, for the most part, are over. Spring is everywhere, in a man's garden and flower bed and dooryard, in his fields, and in his woods.

There is no indecision, a man thinks, in the May green of his dooryard and pastures and meadows. The warm days and the rains have long been felt. The hepatica blooms of April, and the tender bloodroot blossoms, have given way to yellow adder's-tongue and the wake-robin, jack-in-the-pulpit, and the great flowering trillium.

The blossoms of the maple have covered many a roadside and many a hill. The maples, to a countryman, are as beautiful in their spring red as they are in their autumnal brilliance. Bees work among the blooms before they fall in showers in wind and rain. A man feels that it is fitting, indeed, for the maple to usher in the spring in the same rich glory with which it marks the waning of the year. It is the blossom in spring; then the ripened autumn leaf.

71

A man, working his way leisurely through the early May woods, finds the green of the leaves prominent along the woodroads and paths; he recalls his mid-April walk when the rich strains of the song of the purple finch softened the sharpness of the cool spring rain and the wet snow. It is the song of the oriole now, persistent and clear in the forenoon sun; it is the chatter of the barn swallow dipping and diving over the flats of a hill farm. Where a man found the blossom of the maple in April (and even the golden bloom of the witch hazel which seemed to have wintered well through frost and ice and snow and sharp December gales), a man finds the blossoms of the shadbush, spreading canopies of white over the sides of every hill within his view. A man relishes the thought of the delicious feast awaiting the robin in the June shadbush. A man, himself, thinks the flavor is pure and rich, flavored with the crystals of an April stream, and mellowed by the gold of a May sunlight.

THE DOORYARD LILAC

A COUNTRYMAN who has inherited a lilac hedge finds that his uplands are richer by far than anything he could buy. The oldest hedge leads along a stone wall fence by the barn, and reaches on along a quiet lane almost to the slopes of the wild pasture. Here is a richness handed down from one generation to another. Here is a wealth of bloom, and an aroma that fills the air on soft spring evenings in late May and those in early June when the flowers push their spires of purples and whites into the warmth of the year.

There is something about the lilac that always makes a man feel at home, as a woodchuck must surely feel in some deep clover field, or a rabbit in the hillside brushlands. The blossoms and smells have been a part of all his Mays, and he would not dare to guess how many Mays before. There is far more than the beauty of blossoms, more than the rich perfume. There is, too, the loveliness of leaves. A man remembers Whitman's line about the "lilac with heart-shaped leaves."

For years the poets have paid their singing tribute to the lilac, and with anything so homey, there should justly be these songs. A man knows of homesteads, dating back through the generations, some for more than a century and a half, which still have their lilac blooms. He knows of the lilac, growing in the wilderness as it were, where the crumbled walls of foundations reveal that the spot was once a man's home. It is almost lost now in the growth of trees, trees moving in to claim once more the unharvested hills.

The hours are filled with charm when the lilac blooms, when the year touches its warmth over meadow and garden and field. These are the corsages of dooryards and hedges and fence rows. A man will linger long on his way to the pasture to bring in the cows. He will admire the conical-shaped clusters of flowers pointing toward the sky. Others bend downward on the weakened stems. When summer comes, he will linger again in the shade of the tall bushes, some which reach as high as the weathered barns. Robins and song sparrows and chipping sparrows build in the old and sturdy boughs.

A man says his ancestral farm home should forever have its lilacs. So he, too, has planted a hedge reaching almost from his dooryard to a small stream. He has planted lilacs along his creek banks, and in the edge of his woods. He remembers his own tribute to the lilac, one that will in time, he hopes, fit the bushes he has sown "when May brings lilac days and the hedge puts forth its bloom again as it has for a hundred springs."

ALONG
GARDEN WALLS

IT IS the old garden wall, early in the spring, that seems to feel the warming touch of the sun, as if the stones themselves were first to absorb the penetrating warmth of its spreading rays. The delightful melody of the earliest song sparrow comes from the rose and forsythia bushes that reach above the north side of the fence. And it is there, on mornings in April and early May, that white-throated sparrows add their whistled notes to the rich spring chorus of songs.

Scene of the first spring melody in the garden, it is fitting, then, that the first spring green should appear along the old and friendly wall. And on the south side, where the early warmth seeps in, rhubarb pushes through the moist and softened earth. At first, of course, the plants seem to push cautiously through, showing only the rich pink or red crowns of the stalk. But then, as if sure of the season and its sun, the growth is rapid and the leaves begin to form, shiny and green and rough. With the good warming days, the leaves become smoother and broader until at last they spread out far and wide, sometimes drooping heavily, and touching the ground.

The plant that yields the garden's first green is the rhubarb. It offers a sort of permanence and persistence that fits in well with the husbandry of the rugged hills of a farm. Through the summer months, the plants will keep their familiar places along the old stone walls. When rains come, the drops will strike with a splattering thud upon the broad leaves, beating almost rhythmically as the pulse of the rain quickens and then settles down to a steady fall. On hot summer days, the earth under the spreading leaves holds the moisture long after the exposed garden soil has grown parched and dry. And a man should not be surprised, if, on lifting a leaf, he finds in the cool damp shade a giant toad, very much and very well at home.

A SINGING HILL
OF PINE

A countryman who has planted trees across the thin and stony acres of his upland farm for many springs, finds that his hills yield even more richly now than he would have dared to hope when the first open field was closed forever to the mower and the plow. The same meadows and fields from which he harvested the timothy and fodder and grain bear row after row of gracious pines and larch and spruce, trees that reach higher and higher with each growing year toward the warming sweep of the sun.

A man remembers the first few seasons when hardly a tree was tall enough to hold its crown above the grass and weeds. Spring saw the timothy grow; summer saw it come into bloom, and ripen in the field, unharvested. Autumn saw the goldenrod spread its brilliant wands across the browning land. But all the time, the trees were taking hold, establishing their roots more firmly into the soil, sending them deeper and deeper into the earth and in between the stones. The years kept moving on, and the trees at last began to

77

reach above the bushes and weeds and the hay, like uplifted arms, reaching for the light and the rain.

Most of a man's uplands have now grown serenely into wooded hills, rolling hills of trees, trees that whisper and hum and sing when the wind moves in to strum old chords upon the limbs and needles and the boughs. And there are other songs. When these were open fields, a man remembers, vesper sparrows sang across the slopes. He remembers the songs that came from the uplands when meadow larks and bobolinks moved through the seasons of sun. A man still has these songs in the open meadows, fanning out like spreading wings from his old and graying barns down on the flat lands.

It is the song of the hills that has changed. A man will listen for the song of the thrush where the thrush never used to sing. He will hear the spring drumming of the partridge, deep among the pines where the oats and the clover and timothy once grew. The mourning dove will nest and call from the trees across a climbing slope where a man once harvested his hay and his grain, and where he had followed the cultivator day after day through the shimmering summer fields. The grain has yielded to a song. And a countryman knows he can reap contentment from a year as surely as there are wooded hills from which the thrush can sing.

A FIELD OF
PLANTED TREES

A COUNTRYMAN who loves trees will find as much pride in a field of planted pine or maple or larch as he will in his acres of oats or wheat, or in his gardens. He views the saplings, set out in orderly rows on the upland fields, drinking their own good measure of sun and rain. Small stakes have been driven in around the young trees, to protect them from the careless walker or the mower. Each has the bright glow of sunlight on its needles or its leaves, and each in some degree passes on that glow of warmth to every person who goes walking through the farm's young plantation.

These trees, unfolding a new era over a man's hills, already are of sufficient size to catch the webs of spiders in the early morning light. The pearls of mist cling upon their fingers just as they do upon the broader, spreading palms of the pines. A countryman bends down closely to look at them carefully. He views a tree in miniature, for each has its system of roots, its small branches, its needles, or its leaves. Though he cannot detect it, the work of leaf and sun are already going on. Under the hands of the earth and the season, the cells are expanding the leaf veins, the roots are reaching deeper into the earth, becoming a firmer part of hills with the passing days.

A countryman can evision an embryo woodland on his upland fields. In these tiny forms half hidden by grass and berry bushes, there will come a day when the shadows will be deep and thick. The branches and the boughs will whisper in the wind and they will keep the ground dry from the moisture of a sudden shower. Birds will build their nests in these trees; the webs will hang from the twigs, and there will be a gleam of sun on the highest limbs. Here is a swell of trees, making rich an old farm slope of thin soil and stone.

There will be more music in these woods than winds pushing among branches and boughs, among needles and leaves. There will be more music than the sound of fast-falling raindrops or the crystaled flakes of snow. A countryman's heart already sings as he works his way through the miniature woodland on his hills, just as the trees themselves will sing in the wind of some future bough-rich year.

STONE WALLS

A COUNTRYMAN is glad if some of his upland acres still have their old stone walls. Generations ago, when the land was settled and cleared, the walls sprang up around all the farmlands, and they served well that epoch of good husbandry. The stones were brought up from the tilled acres, laid into fences which divided fields and pastures and farms. Highways were dirt roads winding their way through meadows and woodlands.

When the automobile came into the country, and dirt roads turned into modern thoroughfares, many of the walls were torn down and used for sub-base.

Time has been kind, though, to those stone walls which have stayed. Ivy, wild clematis, woodbine, and bittersweet have clambered over them to find their place in the sun. The four seasons come to them here. There is the fresh green of the new leaf growth in spring. There is the quiet and restful green of the summer roadside. There is the riot of autumn colors in orange and gold, amber and red and brown. There is the winter snow which submerges them in drifts.

A countryman is glad to leave a few stone walls for the woodchucks to burrow under, and for the squirrels to scamper over on their way to the woodlot. He will let the chipmunks find refuge there. He will leave them as a relic of the days when the land was cleared. He will leave his stone walls in the hands of the centuries for the ivy and bittersweet and creeper, for the moss and the lichens, and for the moisture and the sun.

STARFISH AND STONES

ONE OF a man's most prized possessions is a common sandstone, rich in its rare formations of fossils. It is a rock which actually marks a steppingstone out of the past, far beyond the day of the glacier, and the more "recent" era of the Indian mortar and the hammer stone. It spans the centuries from Paleozoic times to the present. It makes a man's hills seem even more ancient when he takes into account the centuries of their old and historic existence.

A man has always liked stones, and to work among them. He has enjoyed endlessly the building of walls, and the beauty of them along roads, and around pasture and field. He has handled stones when the frost would nip at his fingers, and when the heat of the summer sun would reach up from them to sweep in permeating waves around his hands. He has seen stones sparkle with frost, and steam in the coolness of the sudden summer shower. He has handled loads of stones, and his watchful eye has yielded more than one surprise.

There is the Indian mortar which found its way out of a nearby wall that reached in quietness across the slopes. The worn stone bowl, which held the Red Man's grain, now holds water for a countryman's dooryard birds. It rests in all its splendor on top of a tall stone cairn. Here the goldfinch comes to dip in the liquid coolness in the shelter and shade of the spreading woodbine leaves.

Out in the pasture there are boulders, huge and hard and round, carried in by the glacier. They seem warm in their ancient friendliness. A countryman will go to them often on soft still evenings; he will wait there for the late shadows to move down in all their glory from the sweep of the hills. All around him he feels the serene touch of a setting sun. The evening song of birds yields the richest kind of recessional to the day's fast ebbing glow.

Still, the greatest harvest may be the one common stone with its starfish fossil, formed in that remote era of the ages when great areas of land appeared on the Continent. And there were trilobites and cystoids. This one rare fossil links the hills thousands of years back into the dim and clouded past. A countryman picked the stone from an old wall fence on the fringe of his upland farm. He does not regret that some early settler, in clearing the fields and building fences, had placed the stone in the wall, unaware of this heritage of the ages that had slipped between his hands.

A man has vowed, and rightfully so, that any stone he sees will always be worth the extra effort of deeper and more careful study. It does not matter if it takes another day to build a wall, or to clear a field. Nor does he mind that his acres are those of a hill farm, and that his upland fields are not the flat and spreading areas of rich and productive loam. It is thin soil, close to the foundation of hills that he traces back through the centuries into Paleozoic times of the long ago.

SWEET LEGACY
OF SONG

SOMETIMES a countryman is slow in bringing out the lawn mower after a long cold season of disuse. He knows, of course, what the extra effort of pushing the mower through the thick spring green will demand of him, but he also knows that the tall lush grass may well harbor some unexpected occupants. And when it so happens that his dooryard inhabitants include a song sparrow or two, which had taken full advantage of his slowness to build in the protective shelter of the grass and weeds, a man feels that he is richly repaid for any of his tardiness.

Such a man, if he is one who invites the birds to take up tenancy about his house, will go about his work with special care and thoughtfulness, not solely because a late start in lawn mowing means hard and tedious work, but because he knows that the song sparrows like his dooryard too. They may forsake the rose and the lilac and the forsythia for a warm ground nesting site. He has found the song sparrow's nest hidden within ten feet of his kitchen doorstep. He has found the nest secluded in a more remote part of the lawn. And for such nests, he always leaves a sturdy tuft of grass for shade and shelter.

The doorstep song sparrow, a man remembers, became so accustomed to the movement of feet that the woman of the house could, by approaching with caution and care, stroke with her finger the head and the neck of the mother bird while she sat calmly in her nest.

A countryman likes to have the song sparrows move in close to his house. He has known them to "burrow" in the hay on the thatched roofs of his sheds and shelters. He has known them to set up housekeeping in his onion bed in the sun-warmed garden spot. Song sparrows are joyously good as tenants, a countryman says, and he wants them always to feel at home in his garden and lawn and his raspberry bushes. Any bird which can issue so rich a trill from a March hedge, any bird which can sing so delightfully in either sun or shower, is forever granted lease to any spot it chooses from which to author its endless chords and melodies, its legacy of song.

BLUEBIRDS
AND A MAILBOX

A RURAL MAILBOX, unpainted and old, weathered by the hands
of a generation of years, need not be restricted, a countryman says,
to its intended purpose of holding letters and newspapers and
magazines. After watching a pair of bluebirds move in to claim a
nesting site, a man is glad that it was his mailbox, so that he could
yield its tenancy to a pair of birds of deep rich colors and delightful
songs.

And he did not mind at all that the birds' choice had forced him
to meet the mail carrier each morning, so that the rearing of the
young could continue unmolested. Many songs already have come
from that mailbox, a countryman says, in poetic lines and words
and letters. This season, he likes to think, a new kind of melody
will have its origin there.

When October comes, a countryman believes, the liquid warble
of the bluebird may be even richer because of three or four extra
voices issuing a song for the coloring hills, warmed by the sun touch-

ing the woodbine and sumac and aster. And certainly, he thinks, when another winter has passed, he will have every right to expect an extra melody from his March hill of melting snow. He will be glad then to think, perhaps, that the liquid warble he hears may well have had its start from a roadside mailbox by a countryman's dooryard, in the shade of an old maple, where the delightful aroma of ripening wild strawberries rode on the wings of the soft warm wind of a day in June.

THE LADY'S-SLIPPER

IT MATTERS little to a countryman that both the pink lady's-slipper and the yellow are known by other names. The pink lady's-slipper may be called the moccasin flower; and the yellow the whippoorwill's shoe. What does matter, though, a man thinks, is that his woods can claim both flowers. It is a source of delight to any walker to come upon the blooms in woodlands where the trees are full and still in their summer leaf.

And even though his woods are those through which the lady's-slipper "steps" with grace and with charm in every May and in every June, a man, somehow, finds delight and surprise each year when the flowers appear quietly on the carpet of the forest floor. He thinks it is the kind of surprise he knows when he watches a deer grazing in an open field, or in the wild pasture of his upland farm. It is the surprise he experiences when he hears the black and white creeping warbler in song in his beech and maple woods, the same surprise when the call of the whippoorwill echoes through an evening sky across the summer hills.

A man is familiar with woodroads and woodpaths where the pink

lady's-slipper "walks" as a child of the woods. And there is a wild
flower garden, leading from the house to the well, where the yellow
lady's-slipper blooms year after year. He knows, of course, this
plant was brought in by tender hands, and that the effort of those
hands now are the fruits of age-old dreams unfolding in a countryman's yard. The yellow blossoms, he says, turn his garden into a
rich and lovely place, bringing a deep and golden wealth from quiet
woods. There should be a song, he says, for the swollen flower is
like a puffed-out cheek, ready to issue a soft whistled carol of some
kind for the quietness of summer's shade.

SONG OF THE WOODS

No FLOWERS of the woods are lost to a man who will go out into his uplands of trees to meet the flowers there, secure in the soft moist carpets of warmth. A man will walk carefully and quietly, for this is a forest of flowers, planted by the hands of the years. One likes to imagine that the seeds were scattered and sown tenderly over the leaf-covered slopes, along woodroads and paths, and deep among the trees.

The plants and the shrubs seem small and fragile, indeed, when a man takes his eyes from them, to look up inquisitively toward the reaching spires and branches of the beech and the ash and the oak. How fragile and quiet are the blooms when he perceives the strength and the vigor of the green boughs of the hemlock and pine, glistening in the summer's glowing sun.

A countryman knows that the years are good to the flowers. The years yield their endless seasons of growth and their bloom, their seasons of maturity and seed. The years yield their sun and shade, the warmth and the rain. Summer is a new generation of blooms in the wooded hills. Summer is like the sun of a new day that has moved in upon the fleeting footsteps of the night. Summer is good to a man, and to flowers.

A countryman's scraping hoe will resound through the gardens as he plants his peas and his beans; the hoe of the planter of flowers in the woods must surely be a more gentle one. A man never hears it, unless it is the wind, or the whirring wings of birds, or the frisking chipmunks and squirrels, or the softening patter of the rain. A man thinks of the seasons, preparing a bed of flowers deep among the trees where the hermit thrush sings. And for all he knows, the ovenbird will have its nest where the lady's-slipper bloomed. Or maybe the mourning dove will build its home in the evergreens which sheltered the arbutus flowers. A man hears songs in his gardens. The woods must hear songs too, for summer always brings the sun and the warmth to blend soft music with the bloom.

JUNE GATEWAY

THE STEEP and spreading uplands of a man's hill farm seem always to move into their greatest hour of richness sometime in June when the wild strawberry comes into its own across the sloping meadows and the fields. Just as the woodchuck turns to its clover fields, so will a man turn to his uplands of daisies and thinning hay for a harvest that surely must be as succulent as that of the tender clover leaves.

Before the daisy and hawkweed, the field sorrel and the buttercup stepped in to thin the hay, these were meadows of thick tall timothy. And there were lush green clover lands. Of course, a man who would prefer the better crops of timothy and clover would have plowed these fields before the weeds moved in. Even so, the harvest may well be of the richest and the sweetest kind now that the strawberries are ripening in profusion in the grass and the weeds.

A man has learned from experience that the picking of garden berries, large and firm, is a much easier harvest from the systematic rows across the farm's flat lands, but the harvest of the wild strawberry is, he thinks, a richer one.

93

Deep in the summer fields, a man picks his berries. He finds himself in a world of contentment in the weeds and hay. He finds himself in a world of songs, rich June songs that go so well in meadows that are bathed in summer and the sun. A field sparrow's song will pull at his heart as it does at the heart of the year. Barn swallows move in and out of the graying structures at the foot of the slope. They move out over the flats and up over the hills, sweeping through the warmth of soft June skies just as they have done for untold summers of suns.

Certainly, a countryman thinks, if any month deserves its yearly tribute in poetry and song, it is the month of June. Surely, if any berry of the fields deserves its tribute in sweetness, it is the wild strawberry, ripening in quietness in the old thin meadows of the farm. And if any memories may find their worth of preserving through decades of Junes, they may well be those of the long rich days a man has spent in the sun, harvesting strawberries from the hills.

RHODODENDRON
AND PINE

O<small>NE OF</small> the most cherished gifts that could be handed down to a son, a countryman says, is a bed of rhododendron in a garden spot, as circular as a half-moon held in the coolness of the night sky over the rolling uplands. The garden has had its place for decades now by an old stone walk that leads from the doorstep of the kitchen to the dooryard well. May and spring are times for remembering, but a man never forgets, even for a day, the care that a woman of a past generation gave to the shrubs during her long and fruitful walk through the hill of the years.

The rhododendron thrives, growing more comely as the seasons step in upon the land. It has become as much a part of the farm dooryard as the hepatica beds and the ferns, the maples and the elms. And it has grown to be a year-round source of joy and delight to one who continues to follow the same stone walks and the same paths and hills that his mother knew. The shrubs push out their massive clusters of bloom in every July of warmth and sun. They yield a strong and vigorous green through all the year, and even in the long winters of snow.

A man's lasting tribute may blossom in part from this heritage of love, and he makes each day a day of remembering. But it is in the spring of the year that he turns once more to the tending of the rhododendron bed. He wheels in barrels of old and fallen needles from the hill-land pines. He spreads the needles deeply over the soil around the spreading shrubs. He packs them gently. And then he spreads a layer of humus over the needles to help them hold the moisture of the soft spring rains on through the hot summer days of drying suns.

Never a season comes but what a man finds his hours of reflective content. They are remembered hours, revived as many times a day as he goes to the well for a pail of water. This a countryman has inherited—the love and the pride in children and in home. He, too, will leave his heritage. He has planted a pine nearby, so that in some future era, as the years keep moving in upon the hills, the pine will spread its falling needles over the rhododendron bed to yield an endless cycle of nourishment for the shrub and for the flower.

JUNE'S
PASTURE PROMISE

WHILE A SOFT June wind bears the fragrance of the wild rose, or the sweet scent of newly mown hay, or the rich aroma of the ripening strawberry from the thin summer fields, a countryman, walking the slopes of his upland farm, finds the promise of another harvest that is yet to come. Deep among the raspberry bushes that have found their place on the steep sidehills, a man likes to feel that he stands on the threshold of hope, on the doorstep of a harvest that will take him again to the sun-warmed pasture lands.

These acres are good for harvesting. There are the crops of ripened fruit year after year. There are bird songs; they are good songs for summer hours. Off to one side of the pasture, a marsh pushes its lush green into the warmth, and farther up in the hills, there are stone walls and pine woodlands. But it is here in the pasture that the raspberry asserts its right to the year as surely as the yarrow and the everlasting and the thyme, and as surely as the great proud bloom of the thistle on the marsh's edge.

The thorny stems of the raspberry reach out persistently as if to slow the footsteps of a countryman. He would not wish to hurry anyway. Pushing on through the brambles, he likes to take time to listen to the field sparrow's song. He likes to hear the first crickets of the season tuning up in the hills. He accepts the slow pasture ways with the same sort of ease and content that seem to be a part of his Holsteins grazing in the fields.

The berries are still green and firm in these delightful hours of a northern June, but they are ripening imperceptibly under the sun. The developing caps are awaiting their season of maturity when they shall find their way into eager beaks and hands. They are a relish to man and bird alike, and both have found the promise of succulence. Robins and sparrows fly in and out of the thickets; they perch upon the twigs as if to oversee these good sloping lands of richness and flavor. A countryman, too, hovers near like a bird, in anticipation of summer's fruitful days when a new aroma, stalking the winds, lures a harvester into the sun.

WHERE PHOEBES NEST

CREEK LEDGES, green with their lichens and moss and their ferns, dripping with moisture, shaded by the hemlock, the birch and the beech, lure a countryman time and again to the deep gorge that winds its way down the pasture slopes and the wooded hills. They lure the phoebes, too. Creek ledges, like the road culverts that span the ditches and brooks, are among the choicest haunts of this friendly and familiar bird. High above the water, somewhere, the phoebe can build its home.

The phoebe will often nest, of course, as closely to man as the robin and the song sparrow and the swallow. It will seek his farm buildings, his wagon house and shelters and his sheds. But a man, more than eager for an excuse to follow the stream of the upland farm, will walk the creek banks in the gorge to find the phoebe there. Even on the hottest of days, he finds an atmosphere of coolness, reaching up from the depths of the dampness and the shade, and as inviting as the deep and quiet pools. Sturdy and old, the hemlocks tower above the cliffs and the steep wooded slopes. The trees are older, even, than the three generations of the farm's inhabitants.

Under the ledges, where a man seeks respite from the heat of the noonday sun, the phoebe builds, plastering its nest with firmness against the layers of stone. Overhanging shelves of rock shield both the domicile and the young. Here, in the splendor of the woods, what joy must be this bird's to have its day and its night filled with the tireless chords of a woodland stream; it is a bubbling and liquid song, murmured by the water as it moves softly on its way to the sea.

Boys who grew up with hills and wild pastures and summer brooks always knew instinctively where to look for the phoebe's home. A man remembers there was a boy who, summers ago, often took more than the usual time to bring in the cows at milking time. He would take the longer path to the pasture where the cows grazed in their season of content. The shorter of the paths would have by-passed the creek valley, and its ledges and trees. A country-man still takes the longer path to the sloping pasture lands. He wants that time to reminisce and dream. He likes the song of water over stones. Deep in the woods, he listens to the calls of the veery and the ovenbird. A man likes creek ledges, and the companionship of phoebes, building a lasting friendship into the summer of the year.

A SWINGING GATE
AND ROBIN CAROLS

*A*N UPLAND farm and its years have taught a countryman many
of the ways of his bird neighbors, yet summer after summer brings
its surprise, in the unusual and in the commonplace. He finds it
in the season of summer itself when it settles down quietly over the
hills and the slopes. He finds it in the nests of birds, whether it be
in the delicate structure the ruby-throated hummingbird fastens to
a bough over a woodland stream, or in the sturdy house a robin
builds wherever it may find home.

The robin, a man says, is one of his most patient and trusting of
tenants. These birds have built on the projections over farmhouse
windows. They have built on screens that a man's father suspended
from the ceiling of the porch, screens on which a farmer could
spread out ears of popcorn to dry and mature in the sweep of the
winds, sheltered from the dampness of the fingers of the rain.
Robins have built their homes on the "roofs" of woodpeckers' burrows that a man brought in from the woods in March.

Robins, of course, always take up tenancy in the dooryard trees, and in shrubs, some close by the windows and doors. Two of the most intriguing sites selected for homes, however, have been around a man's barns. One year a lumber wagon stood for a while in front of the barn. It stood there long enough for a robin to build between the whiffletrees and the axle. So a man leased his wagon to the birds until the young had flown.

Again a pair of robins cemented their nest with mud to the central support of an old gate that opened the way from a pasture to the road. The gate was closed when the building began, but it was used more and more as the rush of the season took a man out to his fields. There would be times when the gate would stand open for several hours. Then the nest was some distance from its original position. The birds did not seem to mind. Maple and apple boughs sway too in the summer winds. And a countryman is sure now that his swinging gate has also played an undulating role in robin carols.

A WOOD FOR THE DEER

*I*T HAS been more than a quarter of a century now since a country-man has pastured his woodlands. His father had learned before him that cows have a way of browsing off the new growth of young trees, preventing them from reaching up between the ash and the beech and the maple. He remembers helping his father fence off the wooded area, to confine the Guernseys and the Holsteins to the open hilly pasture land.

Still, a man is not surprised, in the least, on his woodland walks, to find the clear imprints of small hooves, cut sharply and distinctly in the softening leaf-mold in the winding paths and woodroads. These tracks, he knows, are those of the deer, and not those of his yearling Guernseys, grazing in contentment on the other side of the fence.

A man's years have covered an era which marked the influx of the deer into the woods and fields of his rolling uplands. He remembers the first deer seen on the farm, and the grace and the charm with which the sleek animals of the hills "cleared" the stone walls and fence rows in their trips from field to field. Nor is he amazed now to find them in the pastures, not far from his sheep and his cows.

In some of the more severe winters, when snows are deep and long, a man's woodland trees may be browsed by the deer, feeding on the more succulent and tender twigs, or on the bark of the young trees. He would prefer, of course, that the deer leave his trees to the seasons and the years. And yet, on the other hand, he finds a measure of consolation in knowing that the deer follow briskly along in the same pasture paths worn by the sheep and the cows, and that they frequently come in close to the buildings to feed from the fallen fruit of the wild apple trees which cling securely to the sheltered knoll above the barns.

GARDENS
IN THE POOLS

*W*HEN THE fast-flowing waters of spring have slowed down at last in their winding and meandering course in upland brooks and streams, and when the tempo of the liquid flow has lost its urgent and torrential drive from thaws and heavy rains, ebbing to a current that is more in keeping with the rhythmic steadiness of the gathering summer warmth, a man expects his brookside walks to unfold countless green islands of frog spawn in the quiet pools and ponds. These floating islands hold within their cells an upland world of chords. A man likes to think of them as gardens of song, gardens of bursting seeds sending up their "sprouts" that will someday yield a chorus through the corridors of the land.

After a winter in which the water has been held in its frosted and icy chains, it is good for a man to walk down the stone steps of the brook, and in the midst of the warming flow of air from the breathing earth and hills, to come upon these floating islands, shining and new. The islands are already occupied. He observes countless darkened spots on the green surfaces; these are the growing tadpoles. The island seems as fresh and new as the fine uncurling fingers of the wood fern on the banks of his forest stream.

Or perhaps a countryman will think of these surfaces of frog spawn as giant ships, their anchors dropped, and the passengers waiting for the hour when they may take their leave of the vessels for woods and tall grass and garden spots. Until that day, suns will warm the decks, and shelving layers of stone will shield them from the winds.

A countryman sits on the bank of the stream to view stirring life in the pools before him. A thousand seeds move in the gardens of the stream. There is the wet whisper of ground in the sunlight, and the water is answering, too. Out of this island of green will come the magic wonder of days. The polliwogs will find their way to the reaches of the pool. They will develop and change; they will yield their songs. It is something, a man thinks, that this garden spot of the brook will give a rich measure of melody to increase the ever-rising crescendo of a hill farm season of spring. The season would not be spring without the chorus of frogs and toads, the shrill piping voices of the peepers, the quacking and croaking of the frogs, or the slow clear trill of a toad.

THE HIRED MAN

A COUNTRYMAN's hired man may be as much a part of the uplands as the seasons of the year which bring the first spring songs
and the summer green, the golden harvest and the drifted banks of
snow. The hired man has as much a place on the farm as the ivy-
covered walls, and the woodbine. He has his fingers on the book of
the days, and he thumbs the leaves thoughtfully through the round
of his daily chores. He has a fondness for the slopes, whether it be in
the season when heat shimmers over the fields, or when the lighted
waves of goldenrod lead him across the autumn hill, or whether it
be in the season when he breaks a path through the first deep snow
to a winter woods.

It does a countryman good to know that one gets up in the early
morning darkness and goes out to the barn to do the chores, milking
the cows and turning them out to pasture before the pink has been
washed from the dawn, before the dew-covered slopes of the north
meadows have been warmed by the sun. There is something a man
likes when he walks out and sees the worker of the fields preparing
for a day on the land. Somehow, the fields are richer by his pres-

ence. This one who piles the haycocks, or turns the furrows, or bends his axe to the woodpile, has a key to the rich inviting doors of all the seasons and the years.

A countryman remembers now a day in a summer that is past. Returning from a walk in the mint-scented basins of the creek, he stopped for a moment to talk with the hired man. It was good to hear slow words about the progress of the fields, the number of eggs gathered from the poultry house, the repair of the farm machines. This man had risen before the dawn and had felt the morning's hay-scented wind upon his face. He knows the intimacy of the bird songs that follow his labor, of strands of spider webs against the sunset sky, of the slow miracle of the curing hay in sun. He knows the endless changes from day to day, and the treasures that hours of peace and harmony may give to a thoughtful heart.

A countryman may make the rounds of his farm; he may touch the heaped barrels of apples or the store of squash and pumpkins, gauge with his eye the clean-cut woodpile that stands as a monument to man's labor. And he knows that the shadow of a man's hand is everywhere; he has touched these apples, trimmed these trees. He has made the farm better by his careful work and his appreciation of the upland slopes. These mountainous treasures of the days have known a kindly man's fingers and the light of his observing eyes. The hired man has found contentment on the hills where birds can sing.

WHEN
RHODODENDRON
BLOOMS

Y EARS AGO, a countryman remembers, his observance of the Fourth of July was of a different nature from that of his acquaintances in the neighborhood. There was, of course, for most rural boys, a day of rest, respite from the hoe and the cultivator, and respite from haying. But those early Fourths stand especially high on the list of memorable days to a farm boy who loved the out-of-doors and songs and blossoms, for they introduced him to the great laurel, or the rhododendron.

The Fourth of July always meant an annual trip across the meadows and fields and far into the woods, to the one spot where the rhododendron thrived, and where it was sure to be in bloom when July came. The trip never failed to yield its expected harvest. It never failed to give even a farm boy something to contemplate in his walk through the warm summer sun.

A man saw some of the shrubs brought in from a remote woodland, and transplanted in the dooryard. The laurel has grown and thrived; it spreads clusters of white across the border of the lawn of a hill farm. Several of the shrubs were planted in the woodlot too, where their blossoms are a part of every summer. They seem as much at home as the veery and the ovenbird in the summer woods.

Some botanists list the great laurel as "rare" or "uncommon" from Ohio and New England to Nova Scotia, abundant through the Allegheny region to Georgia. Naturally, a northeastern countryman takes special pride in his dooryard and upland woods when the great laurel blooms. The lush display of flower clusters, he thinks, has a quiet way of weaving together a man's farm years, of even reaching from generation to generation.

INVITATION
TO MAPLES

A WOODLAND OF maples is moving in on an old garden near a
countryman's house, where for years the family had worked the rich
and level ground. A man has hoed potatoes and sweet corn and
peas. He has hoed beans and cabbage and tomatoes. He has pulled
weeds and picked stone. He has cared for his garden, while the
woman of the house kept a few rows nearest the dooryard for
bushes and flowers and shrubs. There were roses and phlox and
sweet William, poppies and asters. There were pinksters and forsythia, and lilacs.

Then, because the garden was one facing the large west windows
of the ancestral home, a man decided to give the plot back to the
trees. First the grass came, green and tender and lush. Now the
maples are coming in, freely, in the soil where the vegetables grew.
It is a man's wish to dedicate this spot to trees. There are other
fields, he says, where his garden can grow.

Sometime, perhaps, a man says, a generation may be able to walk out again in its backyard to tap the maples when the bluebird thaws the snow. He feels that years ago men must have had the woods close by. There must have been maples, he says. And there surely were men and boys who delighted at the first warbled call of the bluebird, and the rich sweet maple flow. There must have been autumns, too, he thinks, with October colors spreading brilliant hues against the windows of a home in the peace of golden afternoons. And there must have been summers, and bird songs. Certainly, a countryman says, when this once more becomes a woodland by the house, the thrush should come almost to a man's window to sing the summer evening hour into the night.

A FEW STEPS
FROM THE DOOR

WITH EACH year and with each season, and even with each walk
in that direction, a man is more and more impressed with the
beauty and friendliness of the old railroad swamp. It is a mile-long
swamp, and one that he would not trade for any mile of village
street or for any mile of road. In the first place, few walk this way,
except the section hands. Taking the walk at any time of year, a
man is alone. It is one of his favorite walks, and in years of walking,
rarely has he come in contact with man. It is a world by itself, given
over to birds and flowers and water plants, to trees and grass, to
deer, and to the changing seasons and the years.

Long ago, a countryman staked his quiet claim. He likes the solitude it gives. He likes the charm and gracefulness of the tall reeds
and the cattails, swaying in the wind. He likes the songs at any time
of year.

A man does not mind the penetrating summer heat. And even
the sun of winter seems warmer here, out of the sweep of winds.

There are tree-covered slopes on either side; a turn in the valley shields the walker from the sharp north wind. And south winds are always mild, even on a winter's day.

Each walk opens a man's eyes to new things and his ears to new sounds. For the summer walker, there are many blooms, such as the arrowhead and arums, the reeds and the blue flag; the lily and stitchwort and dodder. And there are songs. Here a man comes in spring to hear the first bluebirds singing from the sheltered slopes. He hears the red-winged blackbirds and the song sparrows. Later in the season, he has found the redwing's nest, not three feet away from the rails, in a hummock in the swamp. Day after day he has watched the eggs, and then the young. He has seen the nest sway in the wind as the fast trains whisked by. He has seen ducks and other water birds. He has seen turtles and muskrats. He has seen the deer loping gracefully across the wild slopes, or browsing in the fields of grass and sorrel.

Here are the first wild strawberries, not far from the channels where the muskrats sunned themselves in those first warm days of spring, and where the peepers filled the whole valley with an incessant but musical din. He has heard the veery and the thrush from the deeper woodland not far away. In winter, a man has been comforted by the song of the chickadee and the tree sparrow's call. It is a world by itself, not a quarter of a mile from a countryman's door.

REFLECTIVE HARVEST

IT IS A quick transition from the days of rich wild strawberries to the season of wild red raspberries. It is hardly more than a step, and unnoticed, almost, by the novice, but understood well by a man who knows a farm year.

He is the man who knows those meadows and pastures. He relishes the long June days of warmth and sunlight, and warm rains. He knows the riches hidden deeply in those thinning meadows where timothy and clover are yielding more and more to daisies and sorrel. For years, he has welcomed the coming of summer, the deep tall hay, the profusion of daisies; their rhythmic movement in the faintest breeze that sweeps over the sun-bathed hills, sending their heavy-blossomed heads swaying in unison. Man knows those fields because he has lived in them, and harvested their riches blended sweetly and full of flavor into the ripe wild strawberry.

But those longest days of the year pass quickly; the sun starts its morning climb a little later each day; it starts its descent behind the western hills a little earlier in the evening. The transition is quick, and almost as quickly man turns from meadows and fields to the old pasture lands where the wild red raspberry ripens in the July sun, and where the black raspberry adds to the flavor and zest of rural living.

The harvest may be light as far as raspberries go, but the harvest, nonetheless, can be rich in sun and song. Chipmunks hurry over the warm stones; woodchucks whistle and disappear in their burrows on the pasture slopes; the chipping sparrow sings incessantly; cows move slowly through the summer heat toward pines and shaded pools. Man moves slowly too, from ledge to ledge, harvesting reflectively and quietly.

DOORYARD TENANTS

*F*ORTUNATE IS a man whose dooryard is not far from creek walls and pasture slopes and upland fields, whose lawn is bordered by gardens and shrubs. Fortunate is a man whose dooryard has an abundance of old and stately trees, the generous plantings of his father and his grandfather before him.

It is little wonder, then, in such a setting as this, that the birds move in, to share protection and shelter, to fill the early morning hours with a medley of songs and carols.

Here come the song sparrows and the chipping sparrows to nest in the gardens and the larch, in the roses and the forsythia. The bluebird comes to the gnarled apple tree, or to the old woodpeckers' burrows attached to the veranda columns, and here the house wren comes. The flicker seeks the maples. The Baltimore oriole hangs its pouch-like nests in the drooping branches of the elms. Robins build in the butternuts and the maples, the cedar waxwing in the cedar, the mourning dove in the pines, and the vireo in the tender maple branches. Chickadees rear their young in an old fence post nearby.

A lawn that lies close to stone and has slope enough to drain the

117

sudden summer shower has advantages, too. Such a lawn is alive with chipmunks which dig their burrows between the stones into the earth. Both the old and the young become a part of man's dooryard.

Little wonder that there are songs and activity when the dooryard tenants move in. A man awakens at dawn with bird songs in his ears, and brisk life glides over the grass and on the stone walks and over the creek walls. The wildlife world in which he lives becomes a part of the dooryard that surrounds the ancestral home. He and his father and his grandfather have provided it that way, provided that the dooryard tenants will be birds and chipmunks. They planned that nature should move in close, for then a man can never be alone.

ROADSIDE BLOSSOMS

Nature has a tireless way of creating a masterpiece of floral arrangements along our rural roadsides, throughout the months of growing and blossoming things. It is a steady procession of blooms, one that starts in the early days of spring, and continues through the quietness of summer, into the crispness of the autumn days. The exquisite arrangement continues to appear along the roadsides even after the first frosts have touched the leaves and the blades of the grass.

Nature's flower gardens start their roadside procession with April's green, and the gold of the dandelion, with the rich marsh marigold. May and June move in, and the procession of blossoms brings such plants as the clover and daisy, the black-eyed Susan, the hawkweed, the wild carrot, the toad-flax and fleabane, the wild strawberry. On through the summer the steady march keeps pace with the maturing year. There are the blossoms of the melilot and the wild evening primrose, the steeplebush and fireweed, elecampane and camomile, St.-John's-wort and the thistle. There are the blossoms of the chicory and teasel and wild thyme, the dogbane and the bellflower, the mullein and joe-pye weed, the bouncing Bet.

The varieties of roadside blooms are almost endless, a country-man thinks. Later on, he sees a profusion of goldenrod and wild asters, a second crop of wild carrot, and other late blossomers which touch their fingers of beauty into the brightness of October days, and even into November along old and protected walls. All add color and richness and delight to the days of a country year.

A man looks to the roadsides for a loveliness that is characteristic of his rolling acres, and the seasons that spread a conglomeration of colors, carelessly, yet richly, over the meadows and fields, in a pattern of consistency. A man likes to feel that Nature's tireless hands had moved these old flower gardens up from the fields and the pastures and the swamplands and created a corsage to be worn serenely and proudly on the rim of the ageless hills.

BIRDS
IN THE PIEDMONT

*I*T IS GOOD for a northeastern countryman to put aside his hoe for a few days, to join his southern cousin in a walk through Piedmont fields. This is a different climate, one that has left out of reach of his own hills some of the color and songs. A man likes the stretching woodlands of pine and oak, and the peach orchards, reaching over many a southern slope. He likes the red soil, and the far-reaching acres of cotton and grain.

A man takes up his watch for birds near an old house, abandoned and crumbling, a half mile back from the road. Grain grows where the dooryard once felt the press of walking and running feet. Woodbine reaches high up an old fireplace chimney and over the exposed rafters of the roof where the shingles have gone. Sitting reflectively in the goodness of ripening wheat, a man looks and listens, and a medley of songs moves in around him. There are old songs, and new. There are the same rich notes of the bluebird and robin and field sparrow. There are the calls of the mourning dove

121

and flicker and crow. He hears the chipping sparrow and finds its nest in the woodbine. He hears the cardinal, and notes its brilliant colors against the golden light of sun. Over and over again the brown thrasher calls. He hears the mockingbird, and discovers its nest, too, in an old plum tree by the path. And still he hears another call, that of the quail, and he remembers the last time he heard the bobwhite was twenty years ago at Mullein Hill near Hingham, Massachusetts.

At home again, a man takes up his hoe. All about him is the music of his northern neighbors. But there is, too, the contentment that comes with the memory of southern songs. Somehow, he thinks, the hoe pulls more easily now through the stony garden soil. Somehow, he says, the medley across his northern hill seems even softer, perhaps because he has touched the summer hand of the south, a land gowned richly in greens and browns, wearing proudly its brilliant corsages, and singing softly its old and treasured tunes.

A FARM WELL

A MAN WHO begins his day, and ends it, with a drink from the farm well, renews a friendship with the hills and the earth and gravel and stone through whose seams the clear pure water moves. Literally, he drinks of the hills, for water is the life of the land, flowing through its veins like sap in the spring maples.

There is a stone walk that leads from the farm kitchen to the well. There are flower beds and shrubs along the walk; it passes under the grape arbor which shelters the nest of the chipping sparrow. Then it leads into the open again, and on to the well. When a man rises in the morning, he turns to the east and the sun and the well. When he comes in from work at noon, he pauses again. When dusk comes, he turns once more to the well.

Take a man away from his old surroundings for a while, then let him come back. One of the first spots to which he turns is the familiar well. He will work the sweep, for he has never forgotten how. He will dip the pail deeply into the cool clear water. He will pull the bucket up slowly, and the water will drip from its sides and back into the pool.

The well has a particular freshness to a man when he comes in from the hot fields. He fills the dipper, and steps back into the shade of the arbor, or sits on the huge stone block at its side. He refreshes himself with a combination of shade and coolness, and the heat and the sun of the day. There is a moment for dreams, while a man watches the cool water drip softly upon the sun-warmed stones.

A man treasures his dooryard well, lined with stones carried in from the fields generations ago. Moss has grown over them. And he treasures the unused well house nearby, where, in other years, milk was stored in the spring before the summer heat moved in, and again in the fall before the late frosts turned sharply to ice. The well house, a man thinks, has an established right to its place among the ferns and herb Robert and Virginia waterleaf, close by the well where the woodbine can climb over the ancient walls of stone.

WATER IN THE CREEK

WATERS HAVE a tremendous strength and power in their surging sweep down the hills; they have ripped through solid rock and they have made grooves and alleys in the records of the stones through many seasons. The throbbing flow dwindles to a trickle in a dry summer; it is refreshing then to go up over the cool and moss-covered rocks, and to look at the work that the flow from heavy rains and spring thaws has accomplished here. The thread of this water can sew a song into a countryman's heart.

Though the water is not rushing now in thundering cataracts of foam, still in these quiet pools and trickling streams, a man sees evidences of the thousands of tenants of his upland creek. Minnows flash their silver sides in the sun and whisk away to the cover of the overhanging shelves. From the dark corners of the pools, the frogs keep a watch with their bulging eyes. The creek is a living thing with many eyes. It may be a salamander down from the wooded bank, or a crayfish among the wet cool stones, or it may be the heron wading through the shallows of a vast domain he calls his own.

A countryman finds friends in the creek. The joe-pye weed is here, and the mint touches his nostrils with a keen but pleasant aroma. Jewelweed and columbine guard the rock. The willows take hold, and the ferns creep down the steep banks of the deep gorge. All these things, backed by the friendship of rock and stone, are steadfast in their years. They speak through sun and rain of strength and loyalty. And there may be new things for a man on his summer walk.

The sounds are gentle ones. On the keyboard of the stones, the slight fingers of the water play their familiar tunes. From the depth of the forest on either side of the stream, the wood thrush sounds its bell-like notes over and over again to echo the concert of the upland stream.

A speckled shade is spread everywhere, for the light bores down through the limbs of the overhanging trees. On the steeper bank, where the water has cut more deeply through the hills, the roots of the hemlock hang down; they show where they have wrestled with boulder and stone to find their way into the goodness of earth.

Creek music is an old song, as old as the hills, perhaps. A man follows in the footsteps of the water, a giant that is quiet now. He hears the echo of its melody across the land. This rocky creek is a part of his upland farm, and its tenants and blossoms and songs are a part of him who would walk its way. The creek is a master of moods, reaching out from the wildness of fluent springs to a summer serenity.

WHISPERING
ASPEN LEAVES

MOST FARM men are likely to think of the poplar as a weed among trees. Even a countryman knows how brief a warmth it yields in a winter room. Yet he is reluctant to measure its value in terms of heat and warmth, any more than he would compare to the feeding value of timothy and clover that of the daisy and Queen Anne's lace, and the goldenrod, which claim their place in fields of summer hay. A countryman's values are based more on a goodness in all growing things that find home in his hills.

And so he accepts the poplar, just as he accepts the thistle in his potato field, or the ragweed and the goldenrod and the wild aster in his corn, or purslane in his garden, and even the choke-cherry and the sumac along the fences that mark the boundaries of his farm and pasture lots.

In spring, there are the poplar catkins, bringing something of a testimony in loveliness to the good new season of bloom. A man has watched the catkins day after day, growing almost into a long and fragile fluffiness, tinted with a sunrise pink, to be moved softly, at last, on the sweeping wings of the wind. There is the smooth green-tinted bole of the tree, glistening in the light of the sun through all the seasons, through fall's mellow light, the crystal sharpness of winter's cold, the softening haze working out across the uplands when the cold ebbs once more to make way for spring.

The poplar is a countryman's friend. He has found goodness in it just because it is a tree. And more than once the summer aspen leaves have told a man when he could expect an end to the long August drought. When an east wind works among its leaves, or a south wind lifts the silvered undersides to the fading sunlight from the clouding skies, he detects a clicking whispering, whispering words saying over and over again that a summer rain is moving in upon the hills.

A SUMMER NIGHT

*L*ITTLE CAN be more enchanting than a summer night and a hill. Climbing the soft upland slopes, and reaching closer to stars, a man knows that many things move over pasture and field and knoll in the dark reaches of the air between the earth and the sweep of the constellations. And the brooding eyes of stars look down upon the land.

Though the sky over an upland farm holds countless stars, a man likes to think of planets of another kind under the footsteps of a walker of the fields. He cannot see them in the unlighted rooms of the night hills; yet they are there, hidden by the black shawl of darkness thrown quietly over the gentle shoulders of the land. These are the stars of cinquefoil and daisy, of buttercups and pussy-toes, of columbine and mint. The aroma of thyme sweeps up from the earth and penetrates the air through which a man walks; he pictures in his mind a vivid spreading carpet over the warm hummocks.

And there are deeper stars under the rolling pillows of grass over dooryard and field. The earthworm finds its way through the kind rich soil of the garden. The burrow of the mole bends through the corridors of the ground; that of the woodchuck reaches into an old sidehill, or between the rocks on a steep creek bank, or a thin wooded slope.

A hill is not alone in its quiet watch under the stars. In the cover of air there are whispers of a summer wind playing in weeds and grass and leaves. A bat flies swiftly through darkened space. Fireflies turn on a thousand golden flickering lights over the farm's lowlands. A bird song starts, and then subsides. For all a man knows, a rabbit moves quickly through the brush thicket on the hill, comforted and shielded by the darkened hours while crickets chirp from the pasture's lichened stones.

SUMMER
EVENING'S SUN

A MAN'S FINEST hours may be those that move serenely across
the hills as the last rays of the evening sun spread their long and
golden fingers over the summer meadows and the fields. The sun
and the shadow work hand in hand over the pasture slopes and the
woods. Even the old stone walls reflect the riches of the hours in
these cherished moments when the day nears its sweet and murmur-
ing close.

Some of a man's greatest dreams have found a delightful expression on the ridge of an upland pasture bathed in the glowing
warmth of the summer evening's sun. The vesper sparrow, of course,
sings an old refrain to the ending day. The bell-like flowers of the
wild columbine move in the faintest touch of a wind, breathing in
gentleness over the rolling carpets of grass and fern. The columbine
seems to belong to a pasture, like the cows grazing contentedly in
the serenity of the hour.

Beyond the pasture fence, the setting sun still reaches into the tops of the tall pines, and the woodland of maples and basswood and oak. The sun splashes strands of warmth and light upon the reaching boughs and the moving leaves. Coming from the heart of the woods is a song that stirs a man to deeper appreciation and a richer love. Surely, he thinks, the pine boughs must vibrate and tremble under the bell-like strains of the song of the hermit thrush. Burroughs spoke of the song as "the finest sound in nature . . . It realizes a peace and a deep solemn joy that only the finest souls know."

A man finds peace and contentment on a country hill in the twilight hour. The blooms of the columbine and the bells of the thrush have helped to show him the way. A hill becomes more cherished with every flower and every song, and with every year. The dreams are deeper; they can be as fresh and fluent as the sparkling water trickling in silvered tones from a hillside pasture spring.

WARM SUMMER NOONS

THE WARMTH and depth of a summer noon, as penetrating as the bright August sun across the hills, are so much a part of the content of a countryman's year that he would ask for little more of these still and placid hours. Summer's kind hands are warm with the rhythmic waves of a sweeping sun. On such days, a man looks forward, especially, to his noon siesta, this hour of rest away from his fields of hay and corn, this hour when the mower stands idly in the meadow, or the hoe rests somewhere along a row of potatoes or cabbage or squash.

From his easy dooryard chair, or from the hammock in the shade of the two white birches on the lawn, a man looks out across his fields, hills that he likes to call his own. Yet he knows full well that they belong to the seasons and to the years. It is an hour of silence, almost, and as deep in some respects as a summer midnight. A robin calls briefly from the creekside butternut, or a goldfinch song moves with the bird's dipping flight through the sun. A house wren scolds because a man has moved too closely to its secluded domain in the grape arbor by the well. Bees hum as they move from blossom to blossom among the white clover heads across the lawn. A song sparrow pours out a delightful melody into the noontime hour, and then it stops. Out on the flats, a field sparrow calls. These are abbreviated chords and notes that one hears now.

Summer noons yield rich and tranquil hours. A man dreams in the sun, or he dreams in the shade. All the summers that have been his, step by in softness and in warmth. They move on in a rhythmic steadiness, befitting these maturing days of an old July. A man dreams of the summers to come, and he contemplates the harvests that the years will unfold. His own maturity, he thinks, has come with these same kind years of ripening.

Summer uplands have a way of mellowing a man's philosophy. It is a golden harvest, as rich as his own ten-acre field of oats across the farm's old slopes. It is a harvest of goodness and fragrance, and rich as the golden bloom of the wild evening primrose reaching up in the meadows to spread a delightful and delicate sweetness in the summer hills when the day is done.

SUMMER SUNSETS

THE OLD stone porch on the north side of his house has long been friend to a man. It yields a cooling comfort from the summer heat. A respite there is as good and refreshing as the clear sparkling water of a woodland spring. After his noonday meal, a man stops often before he goes on to his work in the fields. He found it good in the earlier evenings, too, when whippoorwills called from the neighboring woods, and the bell-like song of the thrush rang out in all the clarity and richness that has been a part of so many summers now.

On evenings in August, a countryman draws up his rocking chair in the shelter of the overhanging roof and watches the slow decline of a sun balanced upon the rim of the hills. Both a man and his upland slopes are preparing for the night. It is a fitting end, indeed, to a day of work and of sun. Here a man can think and dream in the peace and quietness of his farm in the hills. He has long realized that one does not have to go beyond his friendly acres to experience the goodness and depth of living on the land. There is enough of experience and change in the seasons and the years on his own and intimate fields.

The sun dips lower in the west, and the shadows lengthen. Crickets call from dooryard and meadow. The tinkle of cowbells sounds out from the pasture slopes. They are restful sounds that come when a sunset bathes the clouds in beauty and color and draws down the curtains of shade upon the rolling earth. One hill is brilliant in the evening's mellow glow; another is dark. Trees and shrubs and flowers know the loosening grip of the light.

A man need not move from his own porch chair to experience the depth and the loveliness of an August sunset. He need not go beyond his own rugged horizon. He is content to let the sunsets come to him. He breathes of the aroma from the fields. He hears a gentle breeze stir the leafy branches of the elms and the long sweeping needles of the pines. The arms of the trees fade gently into the dark. Night covers the meadows and the wild pasture and the woods; darkness moves in to the steady accompaniment of cricket songs, full and deep with serenity.

YESTERDAY'S HAYING

*A*N OLD rural scene is fast disappearing from our great north-eastern farms. Haycocks, spreading their shadows across the new-mown meadows, are becoming as rare in some regions as the once familiar stone walls that hemmed in the farm fields in years gone by. Man will long cherish his nostalgic memories of both.

Hay balers, dumping bale after bale of the newly harvested crop across the wide meadows, remove some of the richness and charm that a field of haycocks once gave to the summer evening land-scape. But, even so, bales of hay, in row after row, reflect the beauty and the richness of the present-day harvest. As many of the old scenes become a memory of yesterday's harvest, so the work of the present generation becomes more simplified. Mowing away hay in the heat of the summer barn will pass; so will the art and the almost endless task of cocking up hay in preparation to hauling the crop to the barn. Passing, too, will be the skill of loading loose hay, building and binding it on the wagon so that it could be hauled to the barn over the sloping meadows without the entire load sliding off the rigging on some sidehill.

Gone will be the pre-sunset scene of meadows of haycocks, but the harvest will go on in whatever way fits the advancement of the era and the generation. All the written words, dedicated to the har-vest, will record forever its beauty and its sweetness. The poet has written his songs; the naturalist and the essayist have written of it. Men will go on knowing the intimacy of the sun-baked meadows, the bobolink songs, the skillful dip of swallows as they sweep and glide overhead, the aroma of curing hay. Haying will long keep man in the fields, close to the heart of the hills, throbbing warmly and almost vibrantly with the pulse of golden summer days.

WILD BLACKBERRIES

A COUNTRYMAN who welcomes the seasons year after year on his hill pastures develops an outlook that is characteristic of the ruggedness and warmth of the hillsides, an outlook that is flavored with blackberries, and tempered with everlasting and goldenrod, wild roses and thyme.

Nothing tastes more delectable than fresh wild blackberries, rich in their ripeness, and as flavored with sun and rain as they are with spring and summer. The blackberry picker learns the songs that fill the summer days about him, the noonday song of the cicada, the grasshoppers, and the chirp of crickets. The notes and chords and melodies of these instrumentalists of the pasture blend in well with hills and pasture streams, and a soft warm wind in the pines.

The richness of the blackberry, the permanence of everlasting, the loveliness of the wild rose and the serenity of the goldenrod link a man to the hills just as the silvered strands of spider webs weave clumps of bushes together. The strands, reaching from bush to bush, shine in the sun like the great steel girders of bridges that span our rivers.

A man feels the permanence of the hills when he spends hours among them in the sun picking wild blackberries, and when he walks the pastures through which thyme has spread great purple mats, soft and lush like a carpet on the parlor floor. Even the hum of bees harvesting the nectar of thyme's aromatic blooms adds something that makes him glad that he is a part of a country year.

A SPRIG OF PEPPERMINT

Summer walks through the farm creek, dried now by the season's penetrating heat and sun, yield a strong and persistent aroma that has a firm and friendly way of bringing back a countryman's memories of his boyhood trips to a main street candy store. His boyish eyes would fill with eager wonder at the striped sticks of peppermint. Even today, a man's eyes fill with the same sort of wonder as he pushes on through the beds of peppermint which have found lush growth and bloom along the banks of the winding stream, and deep in the channels through the earth and the rock.

A man cherishes the fragrance of the plant whose stems jut out strongly from roots that have wrestled for nourishment in the crevices and stone. The mint garnishes this bowl of the uplands with bright and sturdy leaves. It has won its place in the shadow of rock, once pounded and thumped by ice, and turned over and over by the turbulent flow of the water from spring thaws and the fluent April rain.

Here is a spear of bloom in the summer sun, deep in the channel of the hills. Here is the mint aroma, filling a basin of the earth where the strong pushing fingers of the water had worked curving and winding grooves through the slopes. A man knows that the water, with its thunderous and vibrant step, had walked upon these ancient ladders of the land. And still, when the flow subsides at last, and the loud splashing chords turn into a trickle, and less, the peppermint walks forth to spread greenness over stones.

It is good for a countryman's world that these things come in a placid era of the year when the shouting waves of water have turned into a gentle and liquid carol. It is a cooling carol that goes well with the song of the goldfinch over the hot summer fields. The peppermint goes well, too, with the maturing steadiness of the upland summer. In the year's rich quietness, the aroma permeates the air of the August hour when a countryman walks out into the store of the hills for a sprig of peppermint and a song.

A CATARACT
OF FLOWERS

A CREEK IN September may well be a dry one, but even a dry stone-rich gorge can yield a delicate loveliness in blossoms and in moisture-laden greens that find their way through slate and shale and crevices in the stone. As a matter of fact, a countryman is more or less inclined to observe a similarity between the stitchwort and the creek. One sews the blossoms together; the other issues chords from season to season, tireless chords that blend one year into another.

There is hardly a song in the dried creek now, though a man does hear the autumn calls of the crow and the blue jay from the upland pasture. He hears the squirrels scold and chatter from the creek-side butternuts, and the hickories. He hears the chipmunks call again and again from the sidehills of stone. He may hear, too, the gentle trickling song of a miniature stream, spreading sufficient moisture to build a canopy of green where spring had spilled a waterfall. Where the flow pounded in vibrant and thundering overtones in a long past April, a man has found a bank of ferns and moss, building a crown of softness against the layers of shale and rock, reaching from the bottom of the creek to the upper level of the stream above the precipice.

Wild clematis has pulled itself out over the falls. The white blooms reach up above the shelving rock. Queen Anne's lace and joe-pye weed and vervain hold their gracious flowers in the still September sun. The yellow of the goldenrod has worked its way down from the fields to mingle with the willows and the mints. Stitchwort, too, has sewed its way from stone to stone, and from plant to plant, binding together the whites and the gold, the purples and the blues. It is easy for a countryman to depict a cataract of colors, arched like rainbow hues against the ancient shelves of stone.

There are bouquets now, held in the basins of ferns and moss by the stitchwort and the clematis. But songs will be loud again when the autumn rains have soaked the pastures and the fields, and the overflow starts its turbulent course once more down through the hills. Then, likely as not, a man will return to this very falls, to watch real rainbows in the spray and the mist, rising from the depths of the cataract into the brilliance of the sun.

WINDOWS
OF THE YEAR

A HILL FARM countryman learned long ago that birds and blossoms play musical and colorful roles in the steady progress of the season and the certain sweep of the year toward a golden maturity. September, with its warm days and its crisp nights, heralds a definite turning toward the brilliantly colored days that are stepping in across wood lots and hillsides.

There was a day in August when the crow and the blue jay, calling from the wild pasture pines and the hickories, gave an indication of the fast-approaching autumn hours. Leaves of the maple and the butternut and the elm have long since started their rich parade of color across the slopes. Woodbine starts to spread its brilliant hues over the old stone walls, and to push its bright red spires far up into the branches of the ancient apple tree, and the pasture elms. Thin untended slopes are dripping with the reds of the sumac. Goldenrod pushes its deep yellow along roadsides and fence rows. And the wild aster spreads a deepening purple over the uplands.

A countryman, familiar with the good bright hours of September, knows that the windows of the year are opening wide upon a landscape of color over the wood lots and hills. Where a man looked for the delicate blossom of the hepatica in late March and April, he looks now to the sweeping hues that have touched the woodlands all around him. In April, a man sought the fragrance of the trailing arbutus bloom on a cold north slope; in this September evening hour before the frost, he breathes deeply of the delightful aroma of the ripened grape, an aroma that drifts down from the vineyard and spreads out richly with the wind over a country dooryard.

Songs, too, are building up toward the October crescendo. Crickets will long find a warming goodness in the autumn sun. Katydids will fill the evening hours with chords that are indicative of reflective meditation. The bluebird's warbled note in the forenoon sun is something like the liquid song which worked in over some orchard on a March morning that brought the thaw. A man thinks it is well that the bluebird should close out its year of song over the northern hills in the same delightful way that it ushered in the spring. If a countryman detects something of maturity in the September melody, maybe it is because of the golden setting of a ripened year when fields of cornstalks rustle in the plying winds.

SEPTEMBER GRAPES

To a man who keeps a vineyard near his home, perhaps nothing is more indicative of delectable maturity than the grape aroma that fills the crisp September evening or the fresh cool dawn. The aroma of ripening grapes permeates the air. It is a persistent, yet delicious, reminder of the fast-maturing year.

When grapes begin to color in the sun of warm September noons, a man hopes that frosts will delay their first stinging touch enough for the crop to ripen so that the harvest can be made. Yet, during those days of ripening, he becomes impatient. He stops on the way to the barn in the morning; he picks a cluster of the maturing fruit and eats them, enjoying thoroughly their pure rich flavor, refreshed and cooled by the September dew. He stops again in mid-morning and mid-afternoon, and again at dusk, long after the evening meal.

The days are filled with reminders that summer has passed. The sky and the clouds tell it. Summer's thunderheads give way to high, scattered clouds. The crickets' chorus is an almost endless one. Katydids rasp their chords against the autumn night.

Birds and bees join in the succulent harvest. They puncture the skin for the rich sweet juices. The earth turns, and a man feels that the tranquil summer days are taking leave. New beauty and new flavors and new zest take their place in the farm year.

CREEK-SIDE
BUTTERNUTS

IT IS A delightful farm setting to have a row of butternut trees by the creek wall along a man's dooryard and his garden. These symbols of woods and pasture lands blend in well with an old home, its great lawns and trees, and its stone and shelving rock.

Even before the frosts, the butternuts are ready to harvest. A man knows that he must gather the crop ahead of the squirrels which already keep up a persistent chatter in the nearby trees. He knows that he must work ahead of the heavy autumn rains which will turn the dry creek basin into torrents of water, washing the fallen butternuts under the rocks and into the crevices, and even downstream. He knows it is butternut time when the crows and the blue jays herald the coming of fall from the pines and pasture hickories. A man who has been a part of these harvests since a long-ago boyhood is familiar with the stickiness of the outer jacket of the still green nut, the stains, and the sharp aroma that greets him as he fills the pails. He is aware that the nuts must be spread out and dried before they can be stored in boxes and barrels for winter use.

A man, working among his trees and harvesting the crop, contemplates the rich butternut flavor that blends a taste of the seasons into fudge and nut breads and cakes. He visualizes the deep satisfaction that will come to those who gather on a winter night in the old farm kitchen, where a heaping pan of cracked butternuts rests on the table. He contemplates the real contentment that comes on a winter morning when he watches the chickadees and nuthatches pick fragments of nut meats out of the cracked and broken shells, spread about the sills outside the kitchen windows.

Such a man has long been familiar with the creek-side butternuts, the trees in full summer leaf, or their old and stately forms against the winter landscape. He knows that the seasons will keep on coming to his upland farm, that there will be years of harvests both for him and tomorrow's youth, starting out keen-eyed and eager, with pails and sacks, alert to the autumn smells and colors, awake to every chord and sound of the ever rhythmic hills.

OLD FENCE ROWS

A COUNTRYMAN knows that, in the eyes of his neighbors, his reputation for good husbandry will be lacking if he lets his farm fences grow up to brush; but, for the sake of birds and wild life, he is inclined to sacrifice that "good" repute. The practitioner of good husbandry will, during the wet weather of late summer and fall, clear out the brush along the old stone walls and wire fences that reach like an arm around his fields and his farm. But the man more satisfied with a robin's carol than he is with the extra yield of potatoes or corn, will let the chokecherries and sumac, the raspberry bushes and Virginia creeper, the elderberries and bittersweet, and the ivy, take over their quiet reign. Neglected long enough, these same fence rows will yield their maple and basswood and ash.

It is the old fence row, grown to brush and trees, that lures large numbers of birds before the fall migrations. Here come the robins and flickers, and the song sparrows. On sharp crisp mornings in the fall, the white-throated sparrow whistles his clear rich song.

A countryman needs his potatoes and corn, but he needs, just as importantly, he thinks, the touch of the wilds that assumes its place along the old and neglected fences. He needs, he thinks, that last robin's carol, and the white-throat's whistle. And he needs the song sparrows' medley that is sure to come again from the same farm hedge, when the soft fingers of spring turn the ice and the snow into water and flowing tunes.

A GOLDEN HARVEST

THERE IS nothing slow and tedious about the September days in a corn field where the cricket orchestra rises in pulsating chords into the brilliance of the atmosphere of goldenrod and sun. There is nothing disconsolate in the slow beating rhythm, whether it be loud and shrill, or deep and mellow-toned. Nor does a countryman find anything disconsolate in the sound of rustling stalks, moved by the wind, or by a man who works his way in between the rows of maturing corn.

A countryman finds it good to grow just enough corn to lure him back into the farm lots in these crisp hours of an upland September. He knows, too, that the golden kernels of the grain will be a relish for his flock of hens, and, for that matter, for the blue jays which come in to his dooryard trees when winter's colder step brushes swirling snows across the hills.

Cutting the stalks by hand, and building wigwam-like corn shocks across the slopes, a man has long since found that he can harvest from September just what he puts into the autumn hours. Perhaps his harvest will be the beauty of the aster bloom, or that of the goldenrod, or the coloring hills. These are the ripened hours of an upland year; they are filled with the wealth of sun and of song.

Of course, a man has no way of spending all of his days in the autumn fields, but he will devote to them as many hours as he can. He feels with certainty that crickets must find a deep contentment in the sun where pumpkins turn more golden through the passing days. A countryman likes to feel that his home is his shelter from wind and rain and frost. And he likes to think that the corn shocks across the slopes will be a cricket's house or the home of a mouse. No night of frost can be too long; no day of rain can be too damp, nor the wind too cold. A man, imbued with the contentment of the harvest, knows that winds and rains can never chill the hearth of golden memories.

MOUNTAIN ASH

IF A COUNTRYMAN thinks that the mountain ash earns in many ways its right to its sheltered and lovely spot near the doorstep of his farm home, or by the rim of the dooryard next to the lane, there are year-long reasons why he feels that way. In the first place, a man feels that a tree is his friend, whether it is in summer green or in autumn fruit, whether in winter's leaflessness, or in spring's rich bloom.

Late spring finds the mountain ash in a wealth of blossom. The trees are a mass of clusters of creamy white flowers; the branches bend under their heaviness. There is a blossoming fragrance a man likes.

When September has worked its way into the year, the ripened scarlet berries show conspicuously against the yellow leaves. The berries persist long after the leaves have bowed to the fall frosts and winds. And, late in the year, the birds move in close to a kitchen doorstep to feed from the ripened fruit. Autumn and early winters are brightened by the scarlet berries, hanging in clusters from the bending boughs. Days are turned into song by the chirping of birds gathered in festive mood among the branches. A man looks through the year, almost, from the spring blossoms in the dooryard to the September fruit, then to a rich winter carol by the door.

SUN, SEPTEMBER, GOLDENROD

SEPTEMBER'S GOLDEN arms point the way to richer deeper things. An old fence row, lush with goldenrod; the wild sidehills and roadsides, rich in their golden canopies of bloom, yield a brilliant glow that works deeply into the light of hot September suns. They point the way to flaming maple leaves across the upland hills and woods. They point to bronze and purple, and to orange and yellow hues. They point to brilliant woodbine spires reaching high into the quiet fence-row elms. A man is content that in his summer of harvesting he did not mow too closely to the rusting strands and the old stone walls.

September, in all its meaning of a summer's end, and of harvest and maturity, is something more than a serene and reflective close. A man looks now to the autumn frosts, and his wild-pasture trips for hickory and butternuts. He has joy in his heart, for this is a valedictory.

A man will harvest his corn from the fields. He will reap his buckwheat. He will turn again to his autumn plowing, and he will listen to the song of the share cutting its way through stubble and through sod. He will mark his days with cricket orchestras and sun.

He will mark his days with songs, the departing liquid warble of the bluebird, the call of robins from the wild-grape thickets, the shrill cry of blue jays and the hoarse loud call of crows from the pastures and the pines. He will mark his nights with clear bright skies, with gurgling streams and frosts and sparkling stars. It is a summer's end, and all too soon, perhaps, a winter's hour will close in coldly upon the browning land. But before it does, the goldenrod lifts its bloom into the sun, and a man remembers rolling meadows of blooms, and bees lifting their cargoes of pollen from the fields.

In all the reflective dreams that come to a man in the golden autumn of the year, there is something richer and deeper than a leafless wood. There is something more than the browned fields and meadowlands, something more than the ice and the snow and the white-blanketed hills. There is a winter's quietness, a long and sure beginning, the valedictory of greater things to come when the longer daylight hours press their fingers of warmth again into the time of year a countryman knows as spring.

CRICKET AND WELL

THE STARS still sparkle through the dusk of early dawn when a man goes out to his dooryard well for the first fresh pail of water in a September morning's coolness. The dawn already begins to show its rose-petaled hues over the rim of the eastern hills. There is a delightful liquid freshness about the stone-rimmed well and the underground pool, pure and clear. The well is as old as a man's farm. Generations have turned to it through the many thousands of dawns that have come to the land through a century of ownership. It has long been a source of content to the farm's inhabitants.

Crickets, too, find the curbstones a haven of delight. A man is glad they are secure there, among the stones, high above the water and far below the stars. Their presence yields hours of music in the darkness before the dawn. Approaching the well, a countryman hears the cricket's song, a song that seems more mellow in the stone-lined mouth of the pool. Stepping up to the well, the song subsides, and a man plunges his bucket into the bubbling basin of water. The well-sweep, which has been pointing silently toward the stars, bows to the well, and the pail fills. Raising the pail, the water gurgles and splashes in the pool, and drips against the stones.

With his pail filled, a man takes leave. He has harvested from the treasures of the earth. The fingers of the dawn have not yet put to flight the morning stars. Passing under the arbor where the ripening grapes mingle silently with the September hour, he is aware that the temporary lull in the cricket's song has yielded once again to sound. The steady rhythmic beat resumes; a crescendo of earth finds voice once more among old and silent stones.

RURAL ROADS

To the rural walker, or the leisurely traveler who seeks the country roads along the ranges of northeastern hills, the beauty of the rural road, rich in its October color, offers, perhaps, the last great flow of poetry and song before the November clouds move in, followed by ice and snow. He is like the countryman who has watched his own woodlands turn the hillsides from various shades of summer green to autumn's brilliant hues, and who finds little in the temper of the changing year to lessen the wealth of a spreading countryside of woods and hills. Every year he has watched the change; every year he has found the same richness and beauty, tempered, more softly, of course, with maturity that comes to man as it comes to the year.

There is the amber of ivy with its white fruit, the scarlet and red of the creeper with its blue berries, the delicate wine color of the pinchberry, the brilliant scarlet of the staghorn sumac. There is the brilliant yellow and orange of the bittersweet and its deep orange berries. There is the woodbine which clings and twines to the trunks of trees, extending, in some instances, to the very tops where its red vies with that of the brilliant soft maple. The wild grape, with its large yellow leaves and its purple fruit, spreads beauty to ledges and wild pastures where the bright yellow blossoms of the witch hazel send a golden illuminating light through an autumn afternoon. A man is exhilarated by them.

Back of the rural roads are the autumn woodlands; the ash leaves are brown; soft maples are brilliant spires; hard maples spread their reds and yellows among the woods; there is the yellow of the hickory, the brownish red of the oak, and the endless and persistent green of the pine and the hemlock.

Winter may seem long to a man, but there is something magnetic about a winding rural road that leads on and on in the fall of the year. He cares not where it goes, for, if he assimilates some of the beauty and the richness of it, he knows that he, too, will find the wealth of maturity as golden as the October afternoon, racing toward its conclusion amid brilliant hues on which the autumn sunlight spreads softly its tenderness and warmth. A man sees farther than a boy, like autumn, pointing to something deeper and more rich than the light fresh moods of spring.

HILL-FARM APPLES

A COUNTRYMAN who likes to stay in touch with every phase of rural life will keep on his hill-land enough apple trees to lure him back to the orchards each year. And they may be old trees, landmarks now, that have grown stately and beautiful with age.

Apple-picking comes in some of the finest days of the year, when colors are creeping back into the woodlands and fence rows, when bluebirds issue their last great surge of liquid song before migrating.

A man at work among his apple trees may find that crows and blue jays have been there, that some of the fruit has been punctured by sharp bills. He may find bees and yellow jackets humming in the trees.

Let a man climb his ladder to reach the choicest-colored apples, near the top of the tree where the sun has been most even and abundant, and he finds himself climbing toward the vast clear blue of the October sky. The rich aroma of apples is all around him. This is a delightful harvest, indeed, for the countryman who finds as much richness in October as he does in the April of the year.

He finds this chapter of country living as exciting and full as was the spring chapter to which he turned six months ago.

Old orchards are likely to have Hubbardstons and Greenings and Spitzenburgs, Baldwins and Northern Spies, Snow Apples and Russets. A man remembers that Russets keep far into the next year, and that he will turn last to the barrel of Russets stored in the dark corner of his farm cellar. All winter long man relishes the flavors of hills, crisp and succulent, and the colors, caught and preserved in the skin of the apple. Even the song of the harvest, which pours a fluent melody into a man's heart, will linger through the evenings of snow.

CRISP OCTOBER HOURS

WHEN AN upland summer loses its balance and tips with suddenness into the fall of the year, a new era of frost and color unfolds like a carpet of many hues over the valleys and the hills. The beauty of the autumn-colored land fans into a glowing appreciation any spark of discontent that a man may harbor in his dreams. The change keeps pace with the passing hours. The wind speaks of it more sharply from day to day, brushing a path for the silvered environment of frosted leaves and grass. There is a vigor in the air; the crisp loud snap of the autumn atmosphere is all around, in field and pasture and wood, along a stream.

As if the changing year did not come swiftly enough, rains sweep over the hills and hurry the change along, spreading the flow of color and of frost, keeping in tune with the swiftness of the current of the stream. The liquid fingers of water touch upon the bright October leaves; the hues are even deeper in the golden sun that follows. A countryman is more aware now, after a rain, of the splashing tints of reds and browns and yellows that assume so brilliantly their role over the once soft green of a summer hill.

Unseen pencils and brushes color the land in gowns that soften even the shadows of the night.

A countryman thinks of the change itself as something like the dawn that pushes its way out of the night. There are the deep dark hours. The next thing a man knows, the hour of the dawn has come. And so it is with the season of summer, putting aside its green hills and woodlands for a rich autumnal gown. The thermometer shows less red in mornings now when the mercury dips lower and lower into the realm of frost. A whole new world seems to have moved in upon a man's uplands, overnight.

Maturing apples brighten in the autumn sun. Faint patches of color turn more glossy over the heavy boughs. Autumn has a way of carrying on where summer left off on a hillside orchard. Apples taste better with the progression of the days. Their flavor deepens, as if the fruit itself blended the sparkling moisture from the skies into the tart of the crisp October hours.

MAN, TEAM, AND PLOW

A MAN WHO has kept a team on his upland farm, instead of yielding to the efficiency and speed of the tractor, will find a special compensation in the autumn days when he turns again to plowing. It brings an intimacy with the land that only he can know who follows the team and the plow back and forth across the fields, day in and day out, before the freeze. Even the plow seems friendly, a man thinks, as he grasps the worn handles firmly and almost affectionately into his hands.

A man finds warmth in country living now, for, behind the plow, he keeps on intimate terms with the autumn fields, the bright days of bird songs and cricket calls, of late-blossoming dandelions and speedwell and chickweed, the late goldenrod and aster, and the wild strawberry along some protected fence row. He is on intimate terms with each field and meadow, the stubble and the sod, the contour of his sloping acres. He is on friendly terms with the old grays, plodding along ahead of the plow, crushing the mints, filling the air with a mint aroma that mixes delightfully and well with the rich fragrance of earth. He is on friendly terms with the rock which crops out in portions of the thin meadows.

A man never tires of watching the newly turned furrows, steaming in the sharp morning air while the sun begins to spread out warmly over the upland acres. He never tires of watching the plowshare, shiny and smooth from use, cut its way easily and thoroughly, and with a faint humming song, through the soil of his rolling farm. Each furrow, he thinks, is another in the many lines that must be written across the fields.

Plowing is hard work, but it is satisfying work. It is another in the many chapters of farm living. It is as much a part of fall as the golden leaves of the witch hazel which spread a brilliant golden hue across the pasture ledge to which he looks each time at the furrow's end. Each time there is beauty there. He will not tire of plowing and all that it yields in dreams through the days of autumn sun and clouds. Each fall there is the same enthusiasm and the same delight.

Alone in the fields with his team and his plow, a man watches his upland farm turn from the brilliance of early fall to the brown that precedes the snow. He hears the bluebird warble its farewell song in the old orchard; he hears the robins in the wild-grape thickets. More consistently, he hears the crows calling loudly from the pine woods. Associating these things with his work, a countryman likes to think of fall plowing as a poem of the land; he likes to think of each furrow as a deep and lovely line; he thinks the rhythmic meter is as graceful as the hills of which he never tires.

NO WONDER
A BIRD SINGS

A COUNTRYMAN, wanting to take in all that he can of the year before the long season of snow, will turn often to his fall woods and hills. In these last bright days of color and song, he can think of no richer place than the woods and thickets where the wild grape thrives, where the large vines tangle themselves securely about the trunks and branches and even climb to the tops of the tallest trees for their place in the sun.

It is the wild grape, a countryman thinks, that seems to be enriched by the first frosts, and a man himself, likely as not, will taste of the fruit for some of the flavor that has long since gone from his September vineyard.

A man who likes the familiar calls of the robin and the flicker, and wants still another chance to hear them before they take leave for a southern winter, will be more than sure to look to the thickets and the woods. He likes to have their delightful company as late in the year as he can. There is, he thinks, something about the calls that adds a fineness to the fall days when the colored leaves of the oak spread a hue of bronze over many a woodland.

Chipmunks tell of a man's coming. He hears that constant "scolding" from creek banks and stone walls. Sounding from every quarter of their secure domain in woods and pasture, it reaches a chorus, almost, with sopranos and altos and tenors. While the flickers and robins call from the thickets, a bluebird, winging its way over the hillside orchard, warbles a sweet accompaniment. The large yellowing leaves of the wild grape give a golden softness to a rich autumn medley of songs and sounds. No wonder a bird sings, when the year, growing old, can find its maturity with such grace and such charm.

IN SWEET
FLOWING MEASURE

S WEET CIDER, a countryman thinks, is indicative of something more than a product of the crisp fall apples gathered from his orchards in the valleys and uplands. It reveals in sweet flowing measure the fluent goodness of the land. The orchard has yielded well, a man says, through a season of harvest that had its beginning when the rich flowers were spread in loveliness over the quiet hills of May. Then the orchard was alive with the humming of bees, moving from blossom to blossom, gathering the nectar from the blooms.

Man becomes the harvester in the fall. He will long remember the bright-colored apples maturing in the autumn sun, the pleasant days in the orchard with its good aromas, the fall songs and hues, and the trips to the cider mill. A countryman doesn't have to be old, he says, to remember when he made the trip by team. He says he liked those slow lumbering trips through the coloring countryside, up and down the hills, and over the old plank bridges that spanned the ditches and the streams.

166

Some of the leisure of the old days has gone with an era. But in spite of the quickened pace of the new, once at the mill a man finds the same aroma of crushed apples, permeating the air, and as inviting as ever. He watches the growing pile of the apple pulp. He watches the apples, dumped from the sacks into the hoppers, and carried along on conveyors to the heart of the press. He listens to the crushing of the fruit, and the trickling of the juices as the "jaws" of the press work ever closer together. He watches the sweet fluid creep higher and higher up the sides of the vats.

Sipping the delectable juices, a man thinks he detects something of the hills from which the harvest came. He has a right to think that way. Certainly, he says, a tree, in yielding fruit, draws upon the goodness of the earth. He thinks he detects something of the loveliness and fragrance of the soft spring bloom, something of the deep fresh coolness of a dew under the quiet night of stars, and something of the crispness of fall's first sharp steps across the land.

At Halloween time, a man thinks, when the weird faces of jack-o'-lanterns peer out in startling forms through the darkness of the night from the windows of homes by the road, a man looks back on a harvest that is past. At the same time, he looks beyond the season of pumpkins and shocks of corn in the frosted upland fields, beyond this night of spooks and goblins and broomsticks. There will be long hours of darkness and kitchen firesides; long evenings of sweet cider and popcorn—the long slow evenings of autumn's restfulness. Fall, to a countryman, is the farm year's evening of content.

WOOD-BOX CRICKET

THE COUNTRYMAN, filling the kitchen wood-box on an afternoon in late autumn, has reason to contemplate an evening of contentment in the kitchen warmth where a wood fire crackles and a teakettle sings. But if, by chance, he has unknowingly carried in a cricket along with an armful of wood, he pleasantly becomes aware of an instrumentalist rendering a concert that vies for the best in music of a reflective nature.

A man is glad his day's work is done, and the evening of rest is at hand. Supper is over; he gathers his paper and heads for his easy chair. Outside the late fall chill has at last closed in; ice has formed on the quiet pools. But, by a kitchen fireside, a countryman finds warmth and deep satisfaction.

He reads, then suddenly a concert comes. Slowly and steadily a cricket starts its solo from the kitchen wood-box. The chirp is distinct and clear, and in the confines of the kitchen walls, it has an almost bell-like tone, rich and mellow; none of it is lost in the endless space of the rolling meadows and hills.

All evening long a man rests and reads, and he listens to a combination of kitchen chords. What could be more appropriate, he asks himself, than a wood fire, a teakettle, and a wood-box cricket improvising the autumn day's recessional? He is glad for his good fortune in having brought the cricket into the house as the early darkness came. Nothing could have pleased him more. And he knows, when sleep comes, that it will come with the steady solo of the cricket ringing out clearly and bell-like from the warm kitchen.

THIS IMAGE OF
WOODLAND COLOR

A COUNTRYMAN who has seen the brilliant October colors washed from the fall woodlands by the rain and the wind may turn, if he wishes, to his upland meadows and fields for a plant-leaf coloring that spreads much of the same loveliness in weeds and grass and pasture brushlands. He knows that many plants and bushes provide a recurring color scheme, one that vies with the hues of the October wood lot. Rarely is there any gap to be filled, for one can turn at once, almost, from the woodland colors to those of the pastures and fields.

Patches of wild strawberries, with their leaves brilliantly colored, remind a man of the woods and the pasture where the soft maple and the staghorn sumac are abundant. They are scarlet, and light and dark deep red. Leaves of the hawkweed are bright red and scarlet. The mallow is dotted with a rusty brown.

The leaves of the blackberry provide an image of forest colors, with the various tints of reds and browns and yellows. A man pictures a pasture hillside of blackberry bushes as his miniature woodland, decked out in its vivid colors of fall. The autumn fields are conspicuous with the white seed tops of the everlastings. The fine wiry grass of the pasture lands and the thin fields remind a man of the bright russet color of his beech woods. Grasses in the bogs and the swamplands hold a similar russet, a restful brown.

Many of the greens will continue far into fall. There are the greens of the sorrel and dandelion, the aster and yarrow, the goldenrod and the wild carrot, speedwell and chickweed, spread among the autumn hues like pine and hemlock in the maples and basswood, the oak and the hickory and ash. For the most persistent, a man thinks, there are the leaves of the partridge berry and the wintergreen, greens that will be lost in the snow.

A man who would miss none of the beauty of the October hills would do well to turn to November and its fields for that same loveliness. He likes to think of his fields and meadows as a mirror, holding the reflection of the colors of his autumn woods, like the image of trees he saw reflected earlier in the quiet pools of summer creeks and the ponds.

HILLSIDES OF LARCH

No TREE, a countryman thinks, can be more symbolic of the harvest season than the larch, turning whole hillsides of an upland farm into a yellow and gold that reaches with serenity into the late autumn days, after the leaves have fallen from the elm and the ash and the maple.

There is, a man feels, a definite warmth in such a hill, full and rich in its autumnal gold. It goes well with the farm fields where shocks of corn stand in their brown and silent tribute to fall, where pumpkins smile in the sun, or rest in the sharpness of the star-filled night.

No wonder a man will look often and long toward these hills where he has planted the larch. He has seen the summers of growth and the soft green of the compact clusters of leaves. He sees now this golden hue. He thinks of it as an almost endless flow of color from his quiet uplands, reflected through the meadows and the pasture lands, through clouds and sun.

The countryman is awed by the wealth of his old and sprawling acres. They pour out a golden brilliance in these November hours that step so surely and quietly toward a man's Thanksgiving. He looks; he opens his heart and what he beholds is reflected in his thoughts and his dreams. The colors and the warmth are such that they will be preserved in his album of memories. He will turn to it often in the weeks to come, in those days of leafless winter woods. In his mind, the colors will stay, vivid and clear, pointing the way to the harvest's end, and to the green of another spring. Fall and winter are as brief as summer to a man who is receptive to them, just as the hills and the meadows are receptive to a softly falling snow.

THE SUN
LEAVES EARLY

*I*T IS NATURAL for a man to let his dreams turn to Christmas and the holiday season while he goes about his work around the house and in the November dooryard, preparing once again for the farm year's winter of snow. The air is keen, and a quiet hour is filled with frost. But as the sun reaches higher in the forenoon sky, the frost takes its leave of every blade of grass touched by the spreading warmth across the uplands.

Winter, a man knows, has not yet tipped the scales of the year quite far enough to dump its lasting snows upon the hills, nor to cover the calm and quiet pools with ice. He likes to think of the hour as an interlude, a pause between the final parting of autumn and the coming of the snow.

Every morning the sun is later in pushing its brilliant form over the rim of the eastern hills. The sun is earlier, though, in taking its leave of an upland farm on afternoons. Back in the summer, a man remembers, he could watch the sun go down behind the hills north-

173

west of his barns. Today, the last rich glow comes softly from over the quietness of the southwest woods.

Winter thoughts come easily to a countryman now. When he rounds the corner of the house, he notes the deep red leaves of the dogwood tree, glistening in the light of the midday sun. Most of the leaves have long since fallen, but a few still cling with persistence to the sheltered dooryard tree. He likes to think of it as a Christmas tree, to think of the deep red leaves as the ornaments placed here and there over the outstretched branches. The brilliant leaves sparkle and glisten and shine. He likes to think the glow of the sun is that of a parlor lamp, pushing its rays out to touch the scattered forms, like the ornaments of a holiday tree, glistening in the golden light that reaches softly through a room.

RASPBERRIES AND
NOVEMBER ROBINS

IT WAS A July afternoon, a man remembers, when, with a four-quart pail in his hand, he slipped away from his work in the summer fields, and started out to the brushlands of wild red raspberries. He said to himself then that he was glad to answer the call of the hills, even if another day of weeds did reduce, in some measure, the size of his potatoes, or sapped some of the soil's nourishment that was intended for the corn. Always when he walks away from his work like that, he convinces himself that he can harvest from the crop of wild berries, or from bird songs and sun.

Summer has long since departed from a countryman's farm, but again he feels the same urge to leave his plow. Anyway, he says, his team of grays deserves an "extra" afternoon of rest; the autumn hours of work have been hard and steady and long. This time a man goes empty-handed though, quietly and unannounced, to the same pasture slopes. He knows that any crop he harvests at this time of year cannot be carried back in a four-quart pail. His November harvest will be a hill of bird songs, or the harvest of color from a few straggling leaves that are late in falling or from the deep orange hue of bittersweet berries along the fence, or the color from a few late blooms in pasture and field.

The songs and sounds have changed since summer. A man misses most, he thinks, the field sparrow's song. But any nostalgia that he may harbor for a season that is past vanishes quickly in the autumn sun, a countryman says, when he comes upon a clump of creek-bank bushes yielding both blossoms and raspberries. Almost every fall, he remembers, he has come upon the late-ripening berries, especially in those Novembers when persistent days of warmth follow the first frosts. Though it is something he expects, the surprise is a delightful one.

The "second crop" of wild red raspberries is, by rights, a meager crop, but it is a good one. A man knows there will be no pies from this autumn harvest in his pasture brushlands, nor even a dish of wild raspberries with sugar and cream. Rather, a countryman says, the berries should prove most delectable to a November robin, overstaying its summer year on an upland farm.

IN FURROWS
OF THE WIND

*F*ALLEN AUTUMN leaves seem reluctant, indeed, to stop their traveling as long as there are days of sharp winds and strong gales to push them along on the clear crisp thoroughfares of the air. A man has watched the leaves falling to the accompaniment of the October wind and rain, and in the stillness of the softening warmth of bright sunny days after frosts. He has seen the later autumn winds force them in showers of swirling colors into hedges and fence rows, along walls, and into the pools. They are restless things. Until a snow has thrown its blanket of quietness across the land, they are likely to keep on moving, from roadsides and dooryards, swept on by the surging gusts, and carried downstream by the fluent creeks and brooks.

Sometimes a man, with a dooryard full of leaves, will help them along into his lilac hedge and the corner of the lot. He rakes with the wind, and sends the crinkled forms sailing out on the streamers of the gusts. A man remembers that these very forms, hurried now by tine and wind, once rode the airways of the sun and sky. They once offered canopies of shade under the green of summer boughs. The contemplating countryman will pause from his work. He stands knee-deep in waves of leaves that billow and tumble about him like combers on the shore.

A countryman is invigorated by his work, and by the air of gustiness and disorder, by the tang of the autumn day. From a dark cloud overhead, a squall of snowflakes suddenly sweeps down about him, striking his hands and his face, strumming the dried leaves with quick clicking sounds. He hears the rumble of the wind in the far-off woods. In snowflake and leaf, a man detects the gigantic murmur of a season that is past; the promise of a winter to come.

Bending to his work, a man notes with amusement the antics of the kitten which has ventured out into a tumultuous world of sudden-moving things. A countryman, too, likes the wind, playing in the leaves. He is in league with the forces of the season. He has a share in the long lean furrows of wind that leap across the land. And deep in his world that never stands still, he is making warm the winter of a corner lilac hedge before the upland season of cold and swirling snows.

A NOVEMBER
PANSY BLOOM

GRAY NOVEMBER hours are never without their pleasing and cheerful rays for a man who finds an autumn loveliness in each late bloom that spreads a sunlight of its own over the uplands. He may come upon a blossom along an old stone wall or a fence row, by a roadside, or in a country dooryard. Many a sunless November day has been etched in a lingering smile by the flower of a pansy or a dandelion, a buttercup or an aster. Maybe a goldenrod has escaped the frost. Even the small white bloom of the chickweed in a lawn or a garden may bring something of a sparkle into a countryman's eyes.

Though the colorful season of leaf and bloom has long since come to its end over a man's hills, he will keep on looking for any straggling bloom that the November days might yield. Late flowers, he thinks, are like the warmth of a summer day, reaching on into the night; the heat still holds though the sun has slipped in glory and serenity below the rim of the western slopes. Now it is the year's warmth which yields so slowly to the autumn chill. The summer embers will spread a glowing spark into the snow.

Pansies, warmed by the fallen October leaves from maple and ash and elm, or from the roadside oak, have found an escape from the stinging frosts. They have a way of snuggling closely to the blades of the still-green grass, and the dried and crinkled leaves blown down from swaying boughs. Pansies may unfold their hues of purples and yellows and whites under the shrouded November skies. They may lift the autumn heaviness, like rays of sun pushing warm and brilliant fingers through a thick fall fog.

There is, a countryman feels, an expression of a summer-like persistence in the autumn pansy bloom. A man finds, for instance, some of the same rich colors that were spread in such profusion over the August and September fields. The hues may now be wrapped in the flower of a single stem. He likes to think that the blossom has been imbued with the yellow of the goldenrod, the purple of the aster, and the white of Queen Anne's lace. It is good for a man that a dooryard bloom can hold so much of summer in a gray November hour.

HILL-FARM TENANTS

A MAN WHO posted his woods and meadows and wild pastures when coloring leaves were building canopies and spires of scarlets and bronze and gold across the landscape in the early autumn sun, rather hoped that some of his hill-farm tenants which sought refuge in his uplands would be around to spend Thanksgiving and Christmas and the whole winter season within the borders of his rolling acres. The squirrel and the rabbit and the deer, the partridge and the pheasant, have long been a part of a countryman's hills. He hopes the shelter they seek may be found deep in the spreading plantation of pines, or in the old woods among the oaks and the beech and the green-boughed hemlocks, or in the clearings and pasture lands.

A man who finds richness in the seasons has found that these tenants of the hills are a part of a country year. Thanksgiving could hardly be complete, he thinks, if his acres were not yielding their sustenance to these inhabitants. Perhaps for Christmas a deer will come down from the woods, seeking the frozen apples, long since lost in a December snow under the orchard's gnarled trees. He remembers how the deer came in summer's sunlit forenoons to the salt lick put out for the cows not far from the pasture bars. Deep in the woods, a man may find where the squirrels have burrowed through the snow into the rich leaf carpet for acorns under the trees. Rabbit tracks lead everywhere through the brushland thickets.

Pheasants may find their way out across the snow-covered gardens and the fields. Long after the first snows, old weed stalks reach high above the frozen and hardened crusts. During his winter walks, a man may hear the grouse taking flight from under the snow-covered boughs of the hemlock or a pine.

He hopes his upland tenants will be around to keep him company through all his days in the winter woods. On the day he posted his farm, he detected what he thought was a note of cheerful gratitude in the gray squirrel's chattering. The season is richer by far when a countryman can cherish the companionship of his hill-farm inhabitants, just as he admires the friendliness of a dooryard chickadee.

MUSKRAT MARSH

*I*F A COUNTRYMAN's farm is one of those which holds, somewhere within its boundaries, a stretch of low-lying ground bordering a sluggish stream that winds its way lazily between the sloping acres, he can almost surely count on the muskrat to move in as tenant of the marsh. He knows, of course, that he could dig or plow ditches and drain the swamp, that he could transform the bogs into tillable meadowland, that he could grow potatoes and oats and corn where the reeds and cattails thrive. But if, at heart, he is a wild-life conservationist, he is more likely to let the basin rest in the quiet hands of the hills. He is content to leave the marshland for the muskrats.

A man has seen the sprawling swampland filled, like a dipper, with the heavy autumn rains and the mild spring thaw. He has seen the whole basin turn lush with summer green; then brown as a November field. He has heard the autumn and winter gales sweep the dried grasses, sweep them with a swish that reminded him of a summer field of ripened grain, bending heavily in a humming August wind.

On moonlight nights in fall, he has watched the muskrats at work, building their conical-shaped houses of grass and reeds and roots and mud, building even closer to a man's dwelling than is the house of his nearest neighbor. He has seen these houses hidden among the tall reeds or anchored securely between the clumps of alders and pussy willows. He is satisfied to let the muskrats seek shelter and content in the quiet of their domiciles whose walls turn firm with the winter freeze and from which underwater paths lead out to succulent bulbs and roots in the bottom of the swamp. A man, walking along the shores, hears often the splashing of water as the muskrats move quickly down from the banks or from old logs or hummocks or from the ice ledges where they have been feeding or sunning themselves. He has watched them swim, leaving soft, slow ripples that followed along in the easy-flowing current of the stream.

A countryman likes the idea of having these quiet neighbors near by, safe in their dwellings against the wind and ice and snow, secure in the growth of alders and cattails when summer dips her magic wand gracefully over the rolling hills. In less than a minute's walk from his own dooryard, a man has found his marshland neighbors, writing, as it were, their own lease of tenancy.

ON THIS DAY
OF THANKSGIVING

Thanksgiving, a countryman thinks, could not have found its way into a more reflective time of the year than the late November hour when a season nears its end on an upland farm, and the old year itself moves so steadily toward its certain threshold of history. A man is moved to deep inspiration and devout thankfulness.

It is the farm cellar now which holds the same good flavors that were so abundant in the gardens and fields; it holds the same vivid colors and aromas and succulence that were found in the vineyards and orchards. A man harvested, and the woman of the house, looking to the everyday needs and to family gatherings, canned berries and fruits and made juices and jellies. Farm vegetables, a man knows, retain much of the flavor and goodness of the gardens and seasons. The barrels of apples hold much of the crispness and the tang of October. The cans of berries hold something of summer, and the delightful flavor of the September vineyard is preserved richly and colorfully in jellies and grape juices.

185

A farm Thanksgiving, when a man's family is around him, is indeed an inspiration. It is a good time to reflect on the gathering of crops that is done. It is a good time to look to the sustenance that this harvest will yield through a season of snow. A man's Thanksgiving may have even deeper significance if he is a fortunate countryman whose ancestral home had been handed down from generation to generation. He and his father and his grandfather have been an intimate part of the gentle and sloping lands.

A man can be as provident as his upland farm, and as kind. And on this day, it has long been the family custom to blend into a dinner of Thanksgiving the goodness and the flavors and the aromas of the year. On this day of Thanksgiving, a man can feel the warmth of sunlit fields, and the moisture of rain. He can feel the tender touch of strawberry leaves against his rugged hands and his browned arms. He can see the rhythmic undulation of the tall timothy as the heavy hay bends in a wind that moves so softly across a June meadow. He can hear bird songs and woodland streams; the rustling of leaves in a summer field of corn. Most of all, a countryman says, he has been blessed with the mellowness of maturity in a harvest that now yields its rich and lasting sustenance. He gives devout thanks for the kindness and the wealth of a rich ripening.

LATE DANDELIONS

A MAN WHO, during the spring and the summer, left unmolested in his lawn the dandelion and the chickweed, has nothing to regret in these days, before the snow, when he finds an occasional dandelion holding its golden bloom proudly in the withering autumn grass, or when he finds the chickweed scattering its star-like blossoms in the protected spots in his dooryard. A countryman, in fact, is pleased with himself now that he did not bring out the trowel to weed them out during the tender days of spring when the grass grew lush and rich in the soft May rains. He saw the dandelion turn his spring dooryard into a brilliant carpet of gold. But for years now, he has found the blooms reaching on through the fall, and into the December snows.

It is common enough, a countryman knows, to find these blooms late in the year. Yet the blossoms are something of a surprise to him, or else, he says, it is because he finds so much to delight him in their persistence and their beauty. He is glad that early December days are no barrier to these late and long blossomers. He is glad that the frosts and the late snow squalls have been no barrier to some of the summer aromas, especially that of gill-over-the-ground which has found its place in the thinner parts of the dooryard, close to the shade of the pines, and even under the great spread of the towering elms. He is glad to have found the speedwell in bloom on the border of his garden, the blossoms of the shepherd's-purse, the still-purple bloom of the wild aster, and the swollen leaf buds of the lilac conspicuously green in the hedge along the old lane.

When spring comes again, there will be more dandelion blooms in a countryman's dooryard than he will want to push a lawn mower through, but in these hours, the beauty is something to behold, he thinks, like the glow of a winter sun. The bloom of the dandelion, he thinks, can help light the way through the long gray hours. It is, he says, like an old lamp, turned low, lifting the deep darkness from a man's kitchen, or a farmhouse sitting room.

WARM AS
A MITTENED HAND

SOFT MILD days, warm as a mittened hand, reaching into these weeks that normally would have long since been marked by ice and snow, are a delight to any man who leaves his axe and woodpile for an afternoon's walk to the early winter swamp. He knows that it is usual at this time of year to find the streams coated with ice, but he finds, instead, the running water, silvered in the gold of the sun spread over the hills and pasture lands. He will, of course, find much that is common to any day in early winter—swamp grasses and cattails; osiers turning the border of the marsh into a brilliant red; the black alder berry, a bright red or scarlet, standing out against the brown of the old swamp.

A countryman knows well the tinkled notes of the tree sparrows, which have already moved down from the north. He tunes his ears to every sound or note that issues from the brush thickets, and when he hears the song sparrow in winter song, he feels that it should surely be spring. The melody is typical of that which comes with a warming sun and softens the accumulation of the winter's snow and ice, a song that ushers in the liquid melody of an opened stream. The song sparrow has put a March song into a December hour.

A man, keeping an eye open for all that the swamp and the hills may yield, finds an elder bush in leaf at the year's close. He finds the pussy willow yielding its opened catkins in the December sun. Many are the times, he remembers, that he has taken to the house a twig of the pussy willow, to let the warmth of a room bring out the catkins while the sharp cold enveloped his farm. Few are the times, however, that he has found the December warmth deep and long enough to open the catkins fully, to leave their richness glistening in the winter sun. Now the catkins of the pussy willow spread the blossoms of March over a man's December swampland.

A countryman has found a taste of spring in the December hills and swamps. He will go again and again to hear the melody of the wintering song sparrow, to see the soft catkins of the pussy willow, to touch the blossoms to his hand, though the season of leaf and bloom has long since closed. Such things as these will forever touch a vibrant and singing chord in a man's heart, like a soft south wind, stroking the needles of the winter pine, and heralding the thaw, or like an east wind, touching the summer leaves of the aspen, leaving them quivering and vibrant with life and with song, and heralding rain.

CAROLINA SUN

*I*T IS PROPER that a northeastern countryman, familiar with the changing seasons on his own uplands, move farther afield now and then for a broader perspective of the year's ways, a thousand miles, perhaps, from his hills. Even under Carolina skies, though, a man finds the same reflective moods, the same dreams and thoughts that have been his for so many years in the earlier northern autumn. He seems to feel that the southern fall is a later one, giving him a respite like that of Indian summer over the northlands.

After the leaves of his northern maples have surrendered their brilliant spires of red to wind and frost and rain, southern woodlands continue to spread their hues over a coloring countryside. A man notes in particular the rich and golden hue of the turning leaves of acres of peach orchards reaching on and on over the soft southern slopes.

This, too, is a fall richness, a golden reign, illuminating orchard lands where the ripened fruit was harvested in summer. It yields mellowness to the land as far as one can see. The hue blends a sphere of maturity into the opening cotton bolls, unfolding their blankets of white over the Carolina fields.

Away from his hills, a man still hears familiar notes and songs. Crickets chirp through the sunlit hours, and on into the night, just as the crickets chirped at home. There is the delightful flowing warble of the bluebird, like the one he heard in October over his own steep orchard lands. Robins call from woodland thickets. And there are songs of the south, the mockingbird and the Carolina wren, for instance, adding stranger notes to the same old melodies he had heard from the northern carolers.

Men go about their work of picking cotton from the fields. It is a harvest of the ripened year. There is another harvest, too, one that goes on in its own way over northern pasture hills. Gray squirrels move about the trees, harvesting pecans and acorns and hickory nuts. Blue jays call loudly from the giant oaks. The harvest goes on as a year fades slowly into winter.

This is a sun-rich soil, and the warmth may last longer and reach more deeply into the heart of the earth. But winter will step in at last, stepping more lightly, of course, than a northern December. Yet come it will, in its own way, to the Carolina fields and slopes and woods, just as it is sure to come with sharper step to his upland farm far to the north from here.

It is natural that a southern frost should be much slower with its stinging touch on leaf and bloom. It is natural that a southern spring comes sooner, too. Nevertheless, a northern countryman knows that the fresh new season of song and bloom has always pushed its way northward, through Virginia and Maryland, through Pennsylvania's hills, and on to his own sloping acres, a sweep of rolling land held like a cradle between the Adirondacks and the Catskills.

THROUGH
POETRY AND SONG

Sᴏᴍᴇᴛɪᴍᴇs, the first snow of the season is, in many respects, like a soft spring snow. A man does not expect it to last too long. Yet the winter's fall leaves a different impression upon a man. That in April, he knows, may come in snow showers, clinging to the northwest sides of tree trunks and buildings, spreading beauty in one rich sweep as a finale to a spring rain. The first real snow of the winter, however, is likely to lack that springtime softness.

When the snow comes, a man hopes the hour will find him deep in his woods, or along a brush row, or an old wall fence where the autumn leaves rest in their crispness out of the wind. In such places, a man knows, he will actually hear the first flakes strike upon the leaves. It is music to a man of hills and upland farms. He likes to think he hears the footsteps of winter working steadily across the land. He hears the approach of a season that will push strong sweeping winds over meadows and fields and pastures.

A countryman finds something impressive about a snowfall. He is moved by the flakes swirling down from the clouds of a cold December sky. He is inspired by the deep accumulation which reaches higher and higher over earth and shrub and stone. And a man, years away from his youth, never fails to look back to these earlier years. He remembers the joy it put into a boy's heart to have December bring the snow.

A man's winter joy is in the loveliness of the snow-covered hills, in the songs and calls of chickadees pouring out from hemlock boughs and old orchards, from woodlands and dooryard trees. Whether he hears a chickadee singing in the snow, or a boy, whistling, a countryman finds inspiration, too. He would have this inspiration reach into a soft flowing measure of music through poetry and song.

SNOWFLAKES AND SHEPHERD'S-PURSE

A MAN EXPECTS December to bring the withering grass to the upland fields, and the strengthening ice to the streams and pools. He expects the winds to be keen and sharp, whether they are east winds presaging snow or cold and icy rains, or whether they are northwest winds that herald the bright clear days after a winter storm.

Yet a man keeps a sharp outlook for all that he may find of flowers and blooms clinging with tenacity to some south slope, or in the protected nooks and corners of fences and fields. The season of bloom has long since gone, a man knows, but there are the late stragglers among flowers and weeds just as there are birds which stay behind when the fall migrations are over. Hardly a December comes but what a man sees a wintering meadowlark winging its way over a browned and frozen meadow, or a song sparrow in a thicket of alders and pussy willows, or a robin somewhere in a sheltered valley that borders a stream.

It was a sharp December hour of biting winds a few mornings ago when a man walked out across the dooryard to the mailbox by the road. The wind seemed to brush his face with special sharpness, he thought, until he saw, waving gently in the grass like tiny white flags, the miniature blooms of the shepherd's-purse.

The delicate loveliness of the tiny bloom could well have been lost in a summer season of yellows and purples and browns and whites over the meadows and roadsides of upland country. The beauty could well have been lost, he adds, in a spring lushness covering pastures and fields and woodlands in a variety of color, ranging from greens and whites and blues, from reds and violets, to the rich magentas and the pinks. There will be no clashing of colors, a man thinks, when the snowflakes sweep down to cover the flowers of the shepherd's-purse, waving graciously in the winter grass over a December dooryard.

CLEARING
IN THE WOODS

ON ANY winter's day, a man likes to come upon a clearing in the woods. He thinks of it as a pocket of sunshine resting in the heart of the woodland slope. He finds the sun pouring in to fill the basin with light. It seems as though the golden rays keep flowing in until the brilliance spills from the rims of the cup to spread out softly over the tops of the trees that shield the clearing from the winds.

On a day of fast-moving clouds after the winter storm, a man has seen the sun break through on a hill far to the north of his own wild slopes. And as the clouds moved swiftly on, he has seen the pocket of sunshine dip down to envelop the buildings and meadows and woods, moving across the land as quickly as the sailing clouds overhead. He thought of it as the magic wand of the sun, piercing the overcast to touch its loveliness upon earth and tree and stone. Many are the times he has been in the direct path of the quick-moving light. He could almost feel an instant of warmth and tenderness.

A countryman likes to think that the clearing in the woods yields the same atmosphere as the sun when it reaches down through the cold and broken clouds. It gives warmth to a clearing. A man watches the brilliant light touch upon the red seed cones of the sumac. He watches the brilliance spread its glittering diamonds upon the fingers of the ice and snow. The frost against the glow hangs tiny strands of tinsel upon the needles of the pine. He watches the sun touch the lichen-covered boulder in the center of the clearing, and the snow begins to melt from the sunny side of the stone as if the sun were a warm palm pressing softly enough to turn the snow into miniature streams of water that trickle easily down the rugged face of the boulder.

A man, on his winter walks, will turn often to the clearing in the woodland. He likes its coziness. And if a countryman were a squirrel, or a rabbit perhaps, he thinks he would surely stake his own quiet claim to the comforting restfulness of this sun parlor in the woods.

DECEMBER POND

In a basin of the lowlands where alder bushes and willows and osiers lean in on the crisp December weather, a quiet pond, fed leisurely by hill-farm springs, gives its answer to the changing tempo of the year. A thin coat of ice spreads over the surface of the water, a surface that hardly moves. The pond ripples softly through most of the year except when a flood moves in, or a quick spring thaw sends a turbulent flow rushing down from the melting snow on the hills. In the winter pond, a man finds that there no longer is a vivid reflection of the blue sky and the white clouds, for the tongues of cold have touched these ripples; the ice is closing the windows of the pool against the blades of the stinging winds.

But winter is still young, and the ice is thin. The covering is just enough for a few wind-blown leaves to skim across, and on which the flakes of snow, driven in by a flurry, can skate and slide. In the middle of the pond, there are still open pools. A countryman senses that a frigid shield of ice is spreading out over the water just as surely as the winter night closes in on the day. The air is sharp with cold; the water answers in its quiet way.

Even the open pools in the center of the pond will not remain free for long, for the penetrating fingers of the ice will push deeper and deeper. Meanwhile, a slight mist rises from the fall-filled basin of the land and frosts the alder clumps and osier spires on every side. Bushes are laced and gowned in loveliness; shoulders of frost are held proudly in the gray December hour.

A man knows this time of year as well as he knows the liquid songs of spring. Winter's cold will deepen; the ice will thicken. Next time a man comes back to his lowland swamp, the ice may well be thick and strong enough for him to walk upon. Maybe he can step where he could not go in any other season of the year. Perhaps he can look down through the shield of ice, to the bubbling water in the heart of a country pond, effervescent with a rippled easy flow, far out of reach of the wind and the cold, far out of touch with the snow.

UPLAND THEMES

O<small>N THE</small> <small>DESK</small> pad in his farm library, a countryman jots down notes of the thoughts and the dreams that come to him from out of his hills. Beyond his house, though, the seasons write their own rich words upon pasture and woodland and field. And because a man has read so much of what the years have written across the quiet pages of the slopes, his own themes are, in some measure, taken from this never-ending book of the hills.

Each season writes in its own way across an upland page. Spring's new grass spreads trembling paragraphs in the changing winds. Spring pools leave their liquid messages of rain and melting snows. Every new day enters its record of richness upon the land, distinct and clear as the new leaves that come to a man's woods and his dooryard elms. Woods and pastures, roadsides and fields, are punctuated with a blossoming loveliness.

The writing of the year becomes more profuse when summer comes with its deepening warmth and its lengthening days. The brilliance of the summer bloom adds a touch of maturity to the roll call of the year. The ways of the fields are more certain and serene.

Ripening timothy undulates in the wind as the tall grass bends and sways. Bees hum among the clover blooms. The corn grows and the grain matures. A man roams at will, reading from the prolific lines of this bulging book of summer and of sun.

When autumn comes, the pages turn, and new lines of color are brought out with the goldenrod and aster. The scarlets and golds and the reds and the browns find their way across wooded hills and tree-lined country roads. The sumac lights up its lamps in the thin wood's edge. Woodbine sends up its flaming hues over old stone walls. Fallen apples leave their deep designs in the grass, nipped and withered by fall and frost and freeze.

Winter is forever writing in familiar and picturesque lines upon the land. Rabbits write their essays in the quick or slow ways of their feet across the patches of snow. There are tracks of foxes and squirrels and deer; there are bird tracks, too. All these lines will be folded under by the newer lines of a fresh deep snow. The dark sturdy trees are etched sharply against the winter's landscape and the sky. A winter brook murmurs under its icy covering.

The years write endlessly across the pages of the hills. The lines and the themes may be as old as the slopes and the seasons themselves, yet they seem fresh and new, like the good rich light that comes with the morning sun. They sparkle with the brilliance of stars; they glow with the mellow light that a winter's moon spreads so softly over the December fields of snow.

FARM CHRISTMAS

THERE IS something about the beauty of the winter woods and hills, something about the outdoor winter cleanliness, and the aroma of hemlock and pine and spruce, that works its way into the warmth and cheer of a farm home at Christmas time. A man remembers all the Christmas seasons since boyhood, the flavors and aromas, and the holiday atmosphere. He remembers his father bringing in the hemlock for the holiday tree. He remembers how, as a boy, he and his mother would make their way across the winter fields and pastures to the deep woods, where they would get boughs of the hemlock and the pine and the spruce for decorating the doorways and archways, and for placing sprigs of green above the pictures around the room. The red of the black alder berry was interspersed with the green to add a Christmas hue. Strings of popped corn were looped about the tree to give the effect of snow on bending hemlock boughs.

In the quiet of a Christmas season evening, amid the brilliance of tinsel and illuminating ornaments on which the soft light from the table lamp casts emeralds and jewels, a man feels close to the meaning of peace which the holiday exemplifies. Out of his window, he watches the moon spread its soft and mellow glow across the winter hills and snow. He sees the stars step brilliantly into the stillness of the cold night. He thinks there is something about the comfort and the cheer of an upland home, rich in its setting of greens and reds and whites, something about the atmosphere of the winter night, that speaks out clearly, yet softly and richly, as a symbol of peace.

It is especially fitting, a man thinks, if his own hills are about him. They are the hills in which he has found goodness and peace. They are the hills which have given comfort and content. At the year's end, he can think of no better way to observe the season of peace than to sit back, in quiet reflection, in the warmth of his farm home, flavored with hemlock and pine. He opens his dreams to the broad and spreading slopes under the stars. These dreams are good for a man. He thinks of the snow and the wind and the muffled streams as the psalm of the land, for a farm Christmas, to a countryman, is filled with the love and the goodness and the peace of the hills.

CHRISTMAS
IN AN OLD ROOM

A MAN MAY find genuine pleasure in his farm home at Christmas time, especially if his house is one with an old parlor, a large spacious room with its high ceilings, and its great windows and walls. And he may rightfully find a special pleasure if the woman of the house keeps a Christmas cactus in the room, so that when the blooms appear, they literally fill the corner in front of the relic-cluttered whatnot, across from the antique parlor organ, and close by his favorite horsehair chair.

The blossoms of the Christmas cactus, a man thinks, go well indeed, in the winter sunlight reaching in through the west windows on a December afternoon. They go equally well, he thinks, when there are days of clouds or falling snow, and he looks out of his windows, over his upland acres, and watches the transformation, made so peacefully and quietly over his meadows and fields, over the creeks and the old stone walls.

A man is glad to come in from his work in the winter hills, to the warmth of the room, to find a rich atmosphere of quietness and peace, an atmosphere of contemplation and reflection, etched in the silver of the oldness and the permanence. Everything the room reflects is a symbol of the peace a man holds in his heart, unfolding sincerity and good will and kindness toward men. It is a symbol as rich as the shadow of the button-like seed clusters of the button-bush against the snow.

He finds much of the hills in the old room, and he turns to it as regularly as Christmas comes, just as he has always done since he was a boy. He finds the keen aroma of the pine, delightful as the woods across the pasture and the creek. He finds the brown pine cones, some on the tree, others scattered about the room, on the organ and the whatnot and on the center table. He finds the red of the partridge berry in the half-filled jar of moss; he finds the red of sumac clusters brought in from the clearing in his woods.

This Christmas room is one of peace, a countryman thinks. A farm home offers shelter and song to a man; it yields the carols he would sing for all the world to hear. He would put into these carols the soft rich lines and the contentment and the warmth of an old parlor, the beauty of the Christmas cactus, loaded with blooms, spread like a brilliant canopy over the flower stand in the corner. He would add to this the voice of the winter wind over his home, coming in undulating tones over the hills and the pines, tugging at the windows, swaying the maples and the dooryard elms, then going on its way, leaving nothing but peace in a countryman's house.

A PSALM OF LOVE

*C*HRISTMAS ALWAYS comes to a man's hills, whether a December snow rests in all its loveliness across the land, or whether the frosted fields wait out their hours in the brief December sun. A countryman finds Christmas in the homes of his neighbors and in the spirit of goodness that they bestow upon one another in the certain cycle of seasons that come so surely into the years. Nothing, a man thinks, could be more symbolic of Christmas than a country neighborliness.

The gift of Christmas can have its glowing role through all the year. He has seen Christmas in all the seasons. He saw it when neighbors turned out to help another as the unheralded summer rain threatened a newly mown meadow of hay, or to help sow a field when a spring rain threatened to soak the mellowed soil then ready for the seed. He saw it when they turned out in winter to help a man haul in his firewood, or to shovel snow; or in the fall to shingle a man's barn, or to husk his corn. These are the symbols of love that the meaning of Christmas imbues in a man.

A countryman likes the season of Christmas. He would take from it none of the festivity and celebration, nor the spirit of the Yuletide heard in the singing voices of the carolers and in the ringing of the bells. He would take nothing from a season so blessed with richness and with cheer. But he would add to its festive atmosphere the depth of all that the season yields in neighborliness and in love. It yields a satisfaction and content that blends in well with bells and carols and songs, and with the homes. A man watches the wood smoke rise from the chimneys of those homes; he knows they are warm, for they are homes of love, like his quiet sheltered house among the trees.

There is something in the country kindliness that warms a man's outlook. And he would ask, at this Christmas time, that the country be endowed forever with neighbors and their blessed spirit of goodness and warmth. In his own rich hour of content, away somewhere in the quietness of the hills, he would ask fervently for the enduring peace man seeks and deserves. A countryman would have his Christmas carol a psalm of love reaching eternally into the hearts and homes of all mankind.

EVEN A MAN
IS A CHILD

A COUNTRYMAN has always found a devout peacefulness in his house and on his hills at Christmas time. He has found the meaning of Christmas all around him. He likes the brilliance and the cheer and the warmth of his winter house. But even his upland farm can sparkle and gleam and ring with the joy and the goodness of a country Christmas. Leaving the warmth and the bells and the tinsel that mark the season in his house, he finds the same brilliance out of doors, on a hill, in a pasture, or a wood. Though the hour may be sharp and cold, a man is imbued with the glowing warmth of Christmas time. He hears the bells, too, ringing out clearly and beautifully over the December land.

Perhaps the bells he hears are the tinkled notes of tree sparrow calls from the thicket on a pasture slope. Perhaps it is the song of the chickadee deep among the hemlocks in the woods. Maybe the calls of the season come from the nuthatches and woodpeckers as they move about the dooryard trees. And even more, there is a silvered chord that a countryman likes to hear. A pasture brook, kept open and free of ice by the warmth of an upland spring, sings gently over stones in its softened channel through the snow.

There is peacefulness and comfort in a storm piling its deep white blanket over the frozen fields. There is a contentment in the humming chord of a winter wind. If the day is bright and clear, the December sun slips millions of jewels upon the fingers of the snow. If it is night that finds a man out of doors, and there are stars, they glisten and sparkle and shine in their frosted realm high over the rolling hills.

The red of the sumac cluster adds a flaming hue against the white of a thin sidehill. These are like the Christmas bells hung in the windows of a countryman's house. The twigs of the osier reach like burning candles out of the marshlands. The snow-draped boughs of the hemlock sway gently in all their heaviness. The ice-covered stream, winding down a hill and through a woods, glistens in the sun like a strand of tinsel draped from bough to bough on a parlor Christmas tree.

The peace and goodness of the season walk with a man in every step he takes. There is a sparkling beauty over the December slopes. There is joy in every song and chord. Christmas is in the hills. A man found it as a boy in every winter carol. He finds it now. Even a man is a child when Christmas comes. And imbued with the gladness of the day, a countryman steps more briskly into a winter world. His quickened walk yields a loud crisp song over the frozen crusts of snow.

CHEER IN ONE'S HOUSE

*I*T IS LITTLE wonder a countryman can find warmth in the frozen meadows and fields through which he walks and dreams. A man, on bringing down from his woods a holiday tree for the enjoyment and the pleasure of his family at Christmas time, may well have made his plans to extend the season on through the weeks of snow and cold, through the days when the jeweled fingers of the ice-covered creeks and streams point with a quiet certainty toward the valleys and the lowlands. Making his way across the hill and the wind-swept pasture toward home, a man, likely as not, was thinking then of spreading goodness to both of his families, the one in his house, and his family of birds which has been a part of all the winters he has ever known.

Sometime between Christmas and the New Year, a man sets up a holiday tree for the birds; he moves his evergreen out of doors. He fastens the tree in a sheltered corner of the east veranda, where only the east winds, or those from the south, can tug at its branches. He hangs pieces of suet and old-fashioned "fried cakes" here and there among the boughs.

He knows his winter neighbors will move in then from the far-stretching woodlands of his farm, and from the brush rows, and the thickets. He is just as sure they will find their way to his dooryard as he is sure that water, moving down the slopes and the hills, will sometime find its placid level in a spreading lake somewhere, or in the vastness of an ocean, or in a faraway sea. He is certain of the cheer that will belong to his house, cheer in the song and the friendliness of birds outside his door, songs of these feathered friends of the woods and fields, sweeping now with the wind and the snow-flakes in a man's dooryard.

For days and weeks on end, the tree will stay, and chickadees and nuthatches and woodpeckers will become a part of its spreading boughs. From time to time, he knows, the tree sparrows will turn from the grass and weed seeds to join in the festivities and the songs. Long after a late winter sun begins its sure and steady softening of the snow, and even into April, the birds will come; their melodies will forever be a part of a countryman's winter.

Clearing the paths of snow, or bringing in water from the well, or wood from the shed, or going about the daily chores about an old farm home, a man watches, and he enjoys his outdoor neighbors, the movement in their wings, their small beaded eyes, and their constant chatter, sounding like contentment in the sharp and frosted hours. Looking out his windows in the morning, or at noon, or before the darkness comes, he finds a deep and lasting delight in a tree, a tree alive with birds, and warm with the same kind of friendliness that he has found, deep in the woods, out of the long reach of the ice and the winter wind.